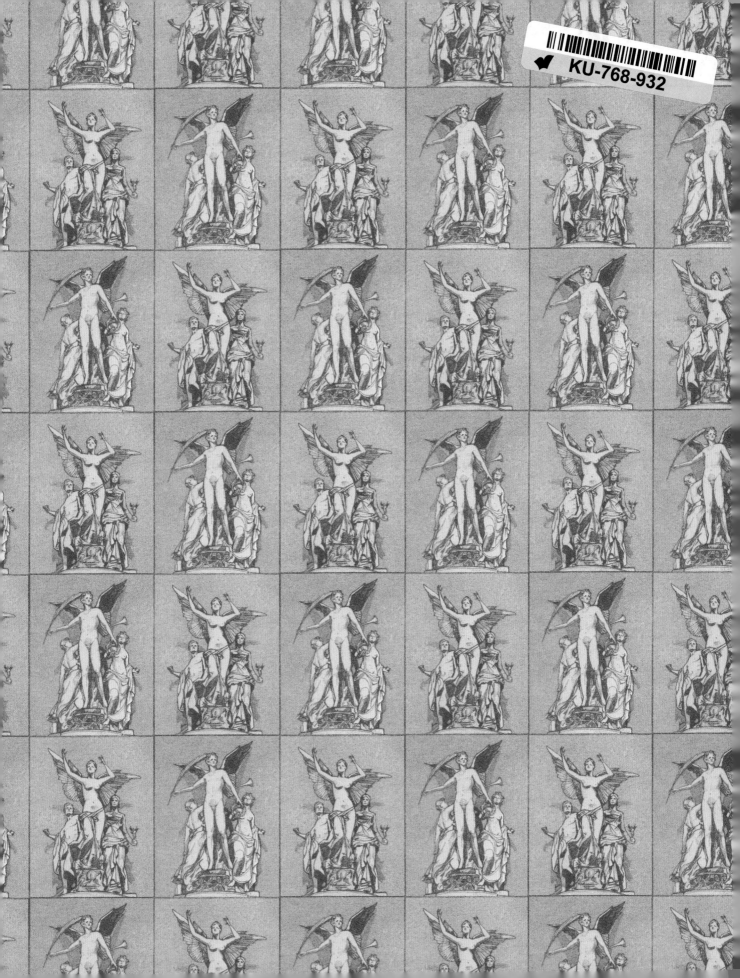

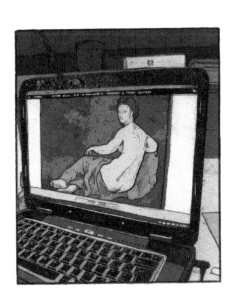

1 3 5 7 9 10 8 6 4 2

Jonathan Cape, an imprint of Vintage,
20 Vauxhall Bridge Road,
London SW1V 2SA

Jonathan Cape is part of the Penguin Random House group of companies whose
addresses can be found at global.penguinrandomhouse.com.

 | Penguin
Random House
UK

First published in Belgium by Oogachten in 2014

First published in Great Britain by Jonathan Cape in 2016

www.vintage-books.co.uk

A CIP catalogue record for this book is available from the British Library

ISBN 9780224101462

Printed and bound in China by C&C Offset Printing Co., Ltd

Hubert

BEN GIJSEMANS

Translated from the Dutch by
Julia Blackburn and Sandra van Beek

JONATHAN CAPE
LONDON

[redacted]

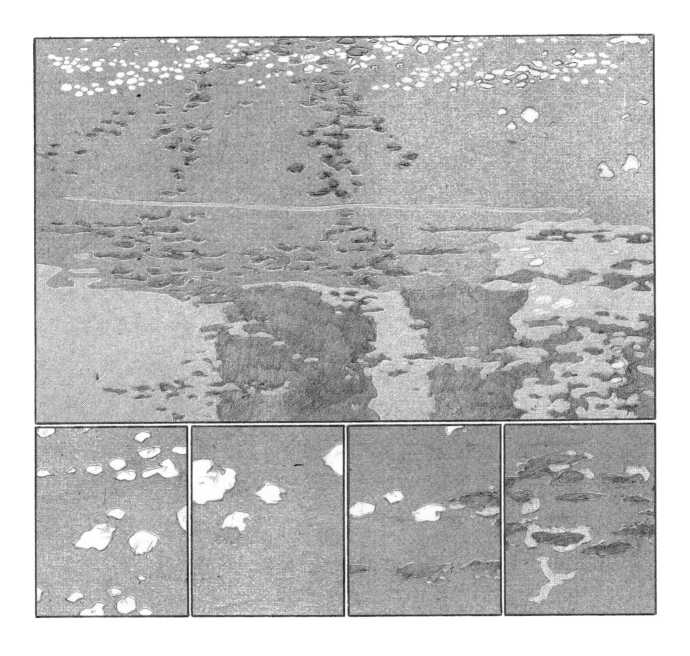

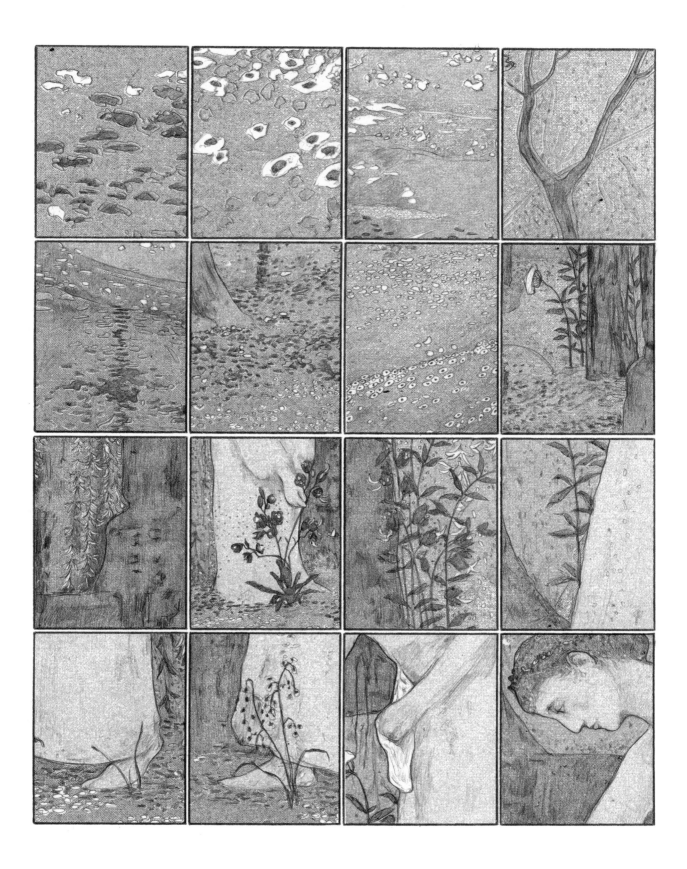

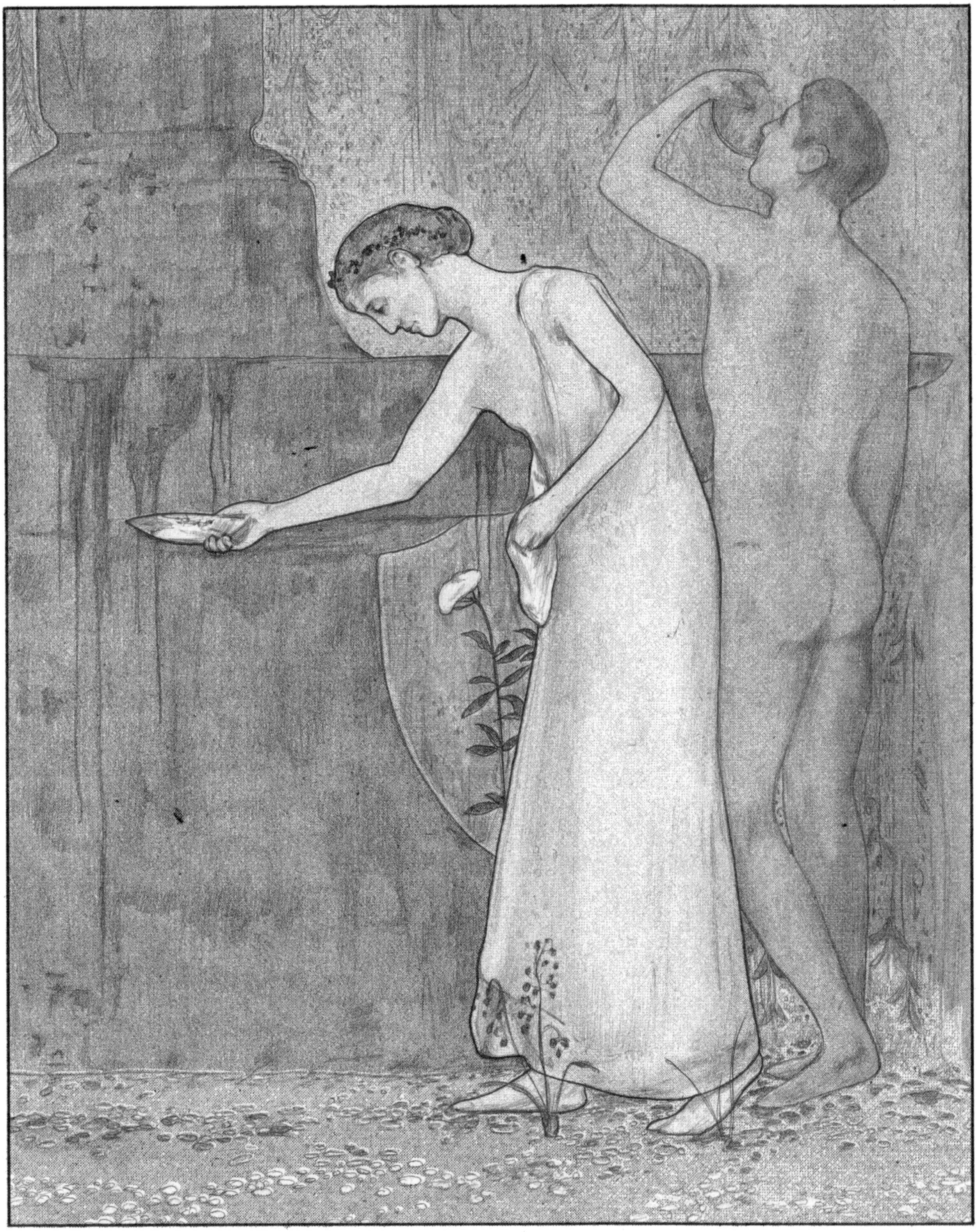

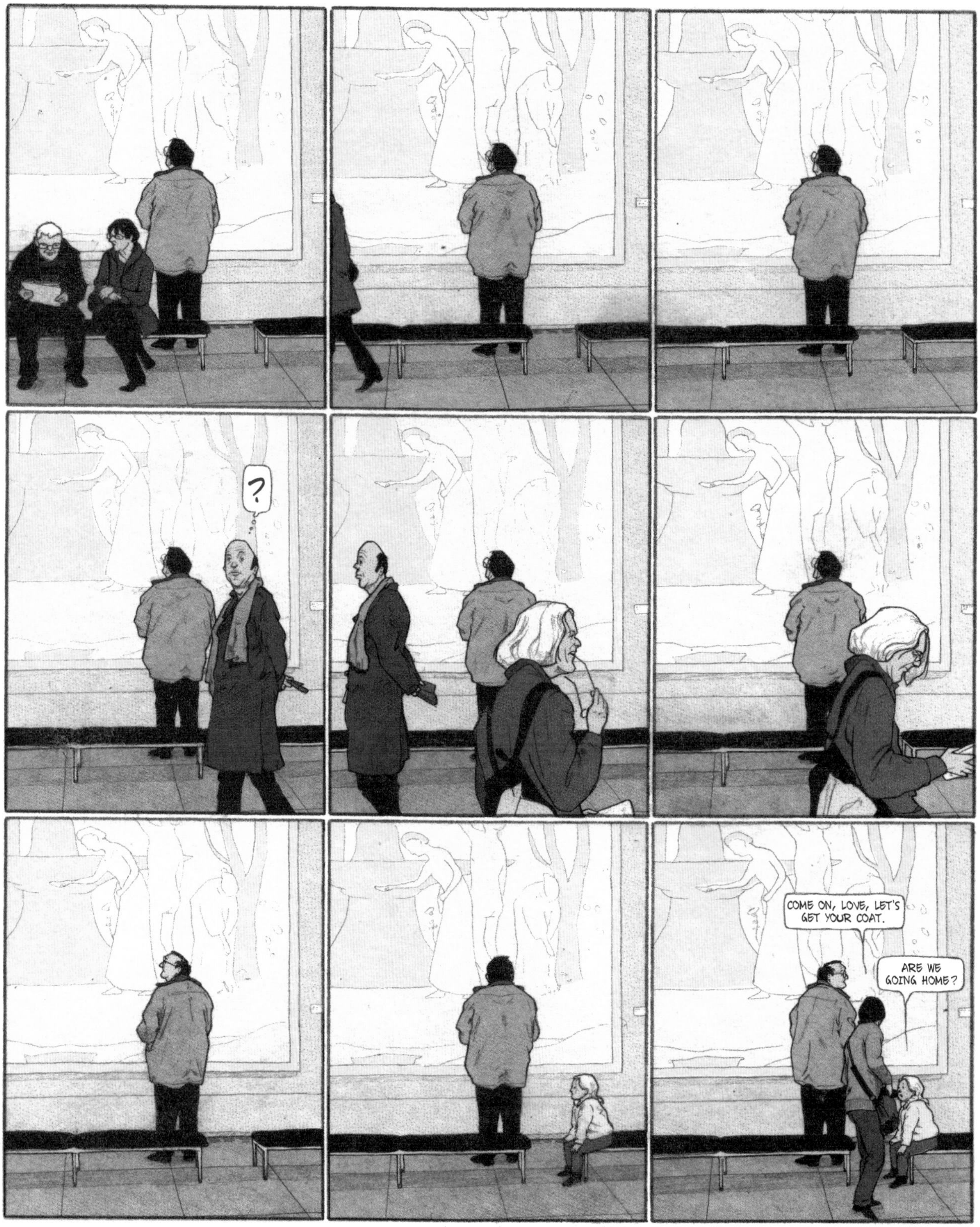
?
COME ON, LOVE, LET'S GET YOUR COAT.
ARE WE GOING HOME?

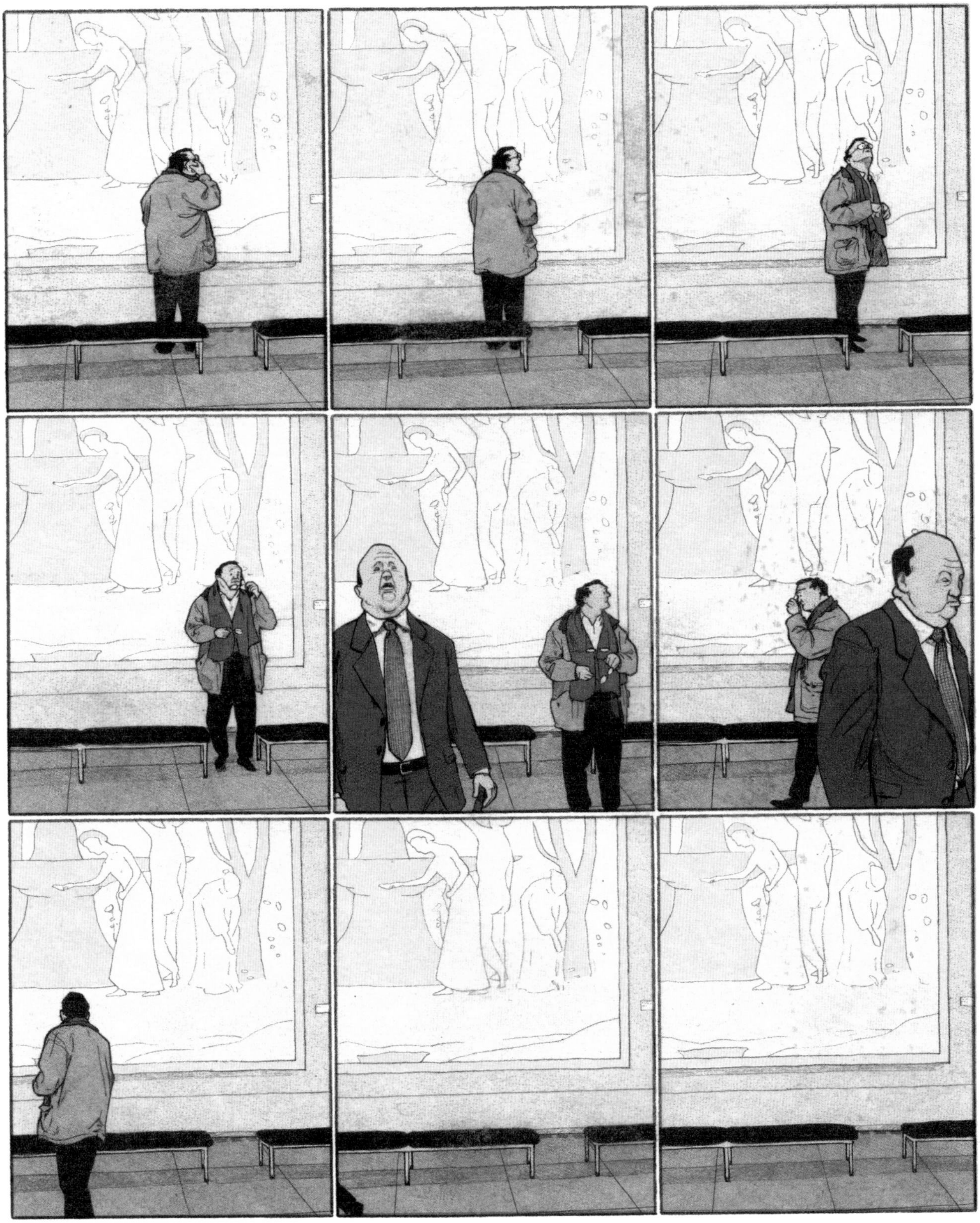

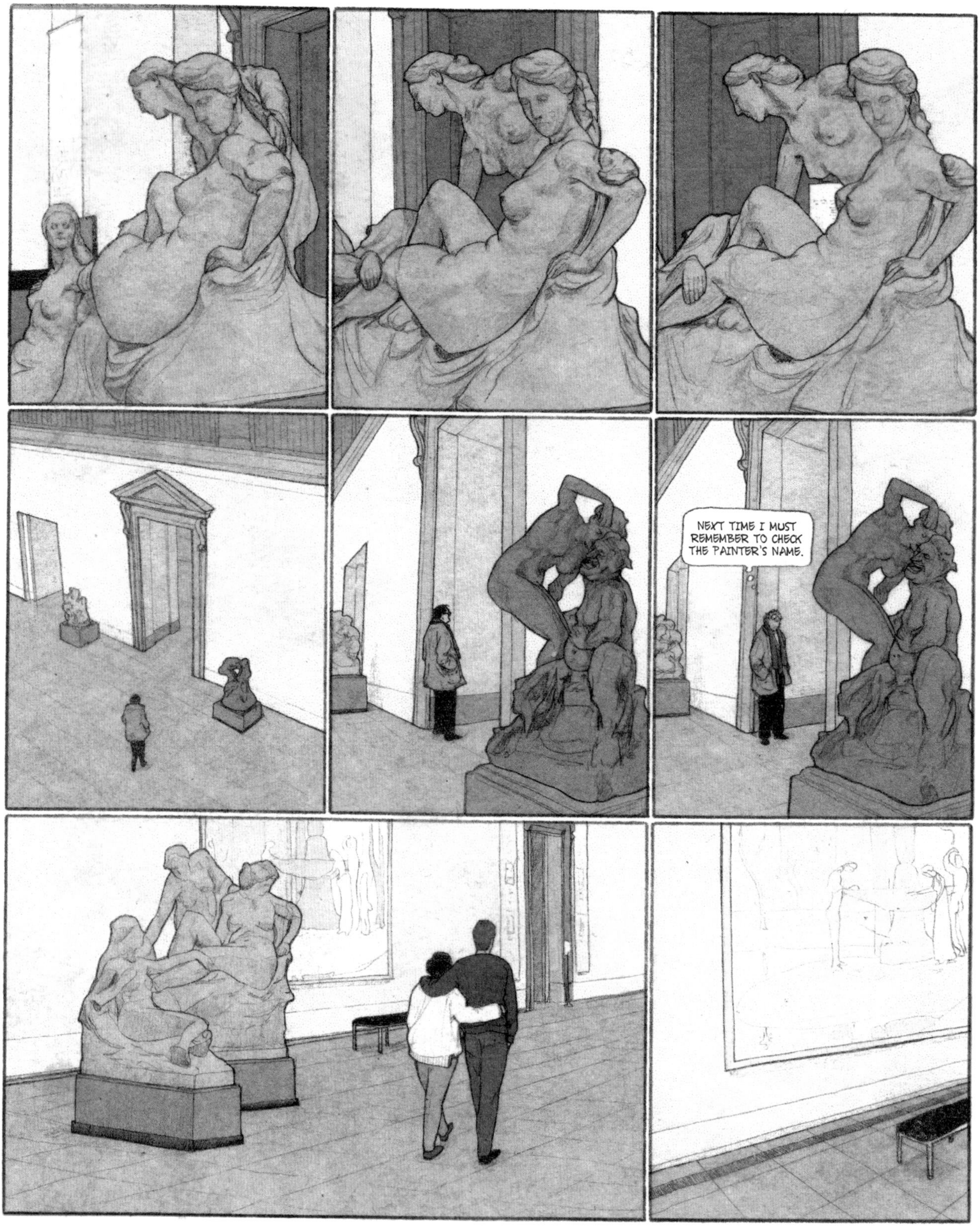
NEXT TIME I MUST REMEMBER TO CHECK THE PAINTER'S NAME.

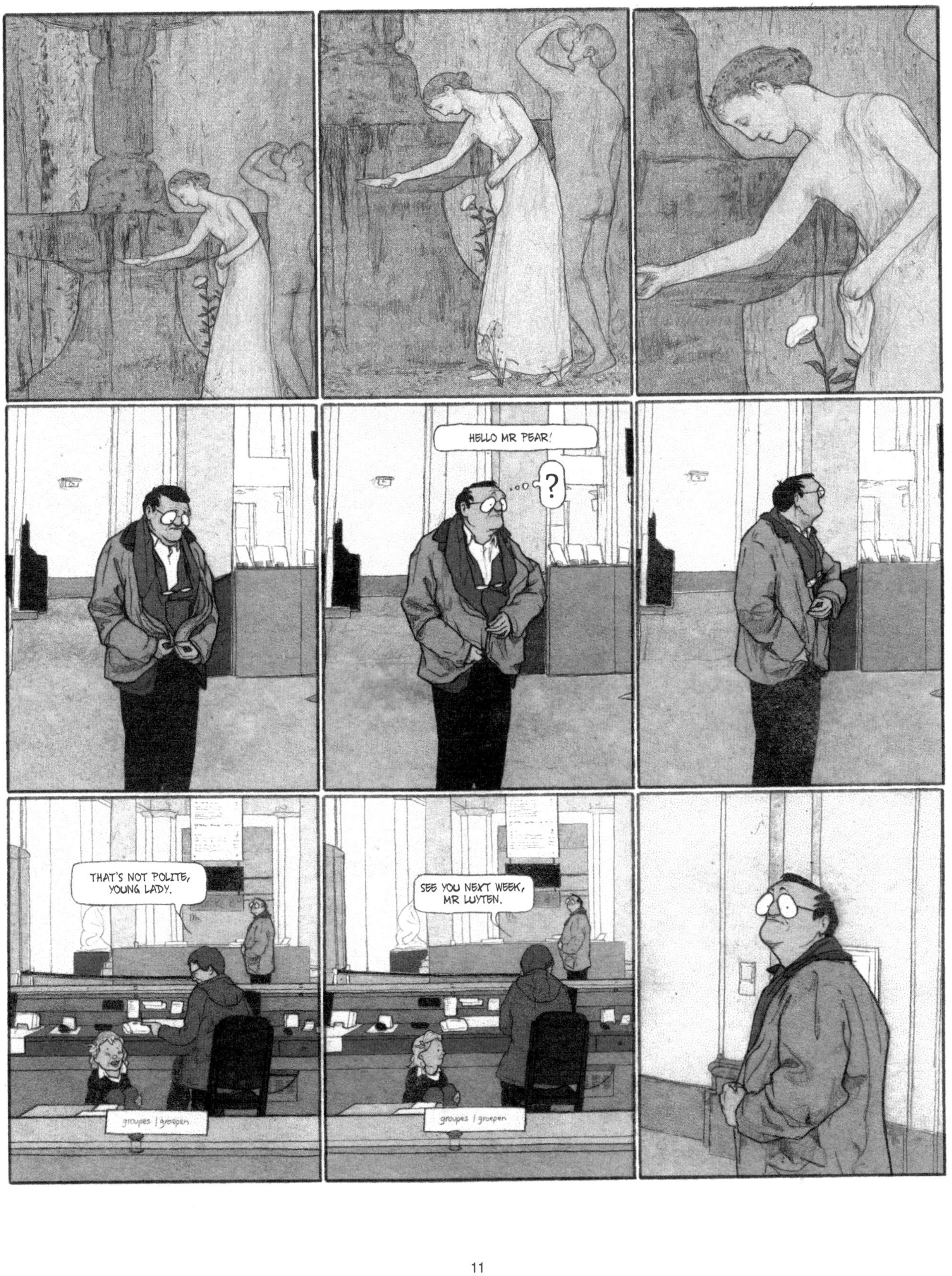

HELLO MR PEAR!
?
THAT'S NOT POLITE, YOUNG LADY.
groupes / groepen
SEE YOU NEXT WEEK, MR LUYTEN.
groupes / groepen

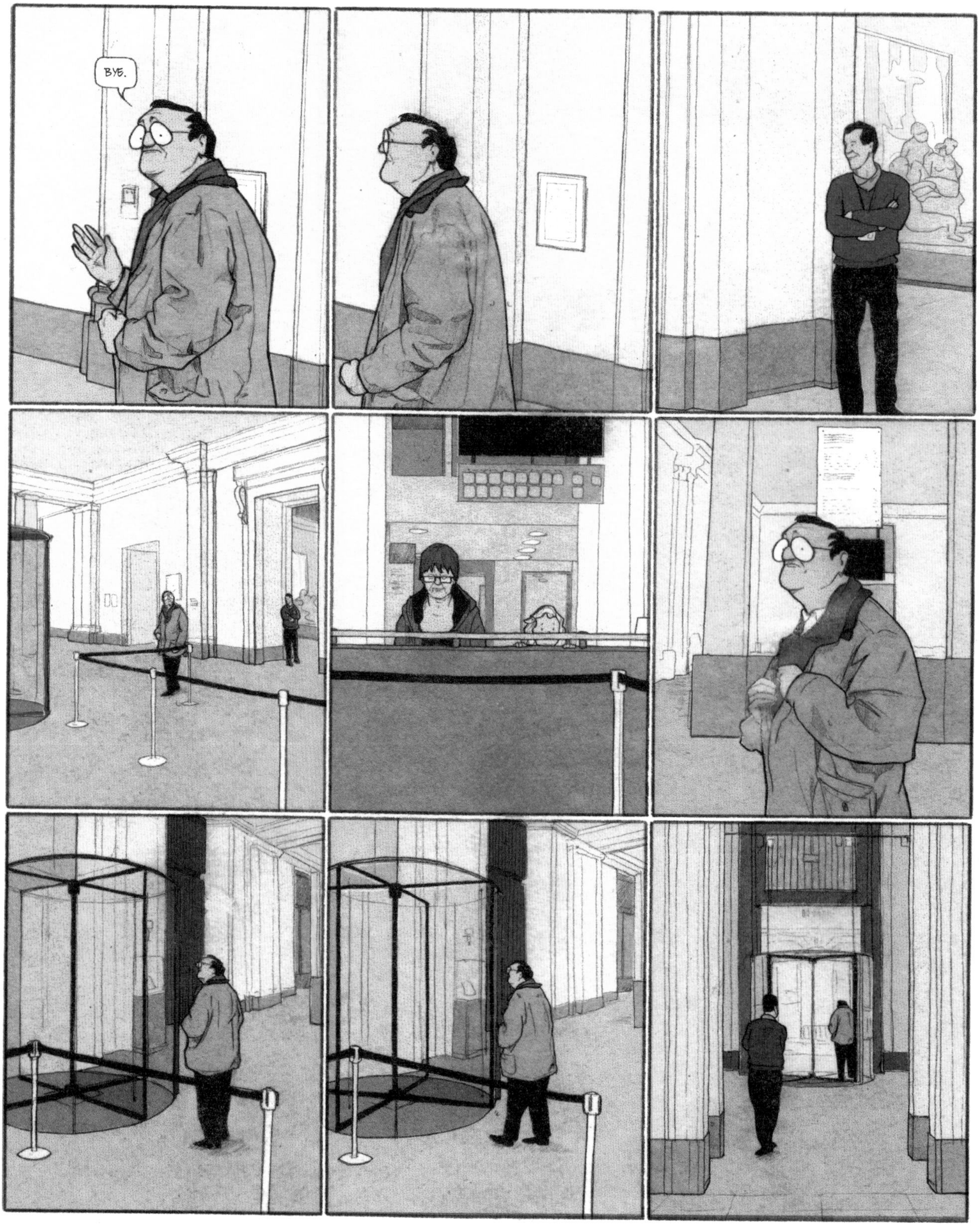
BYE.

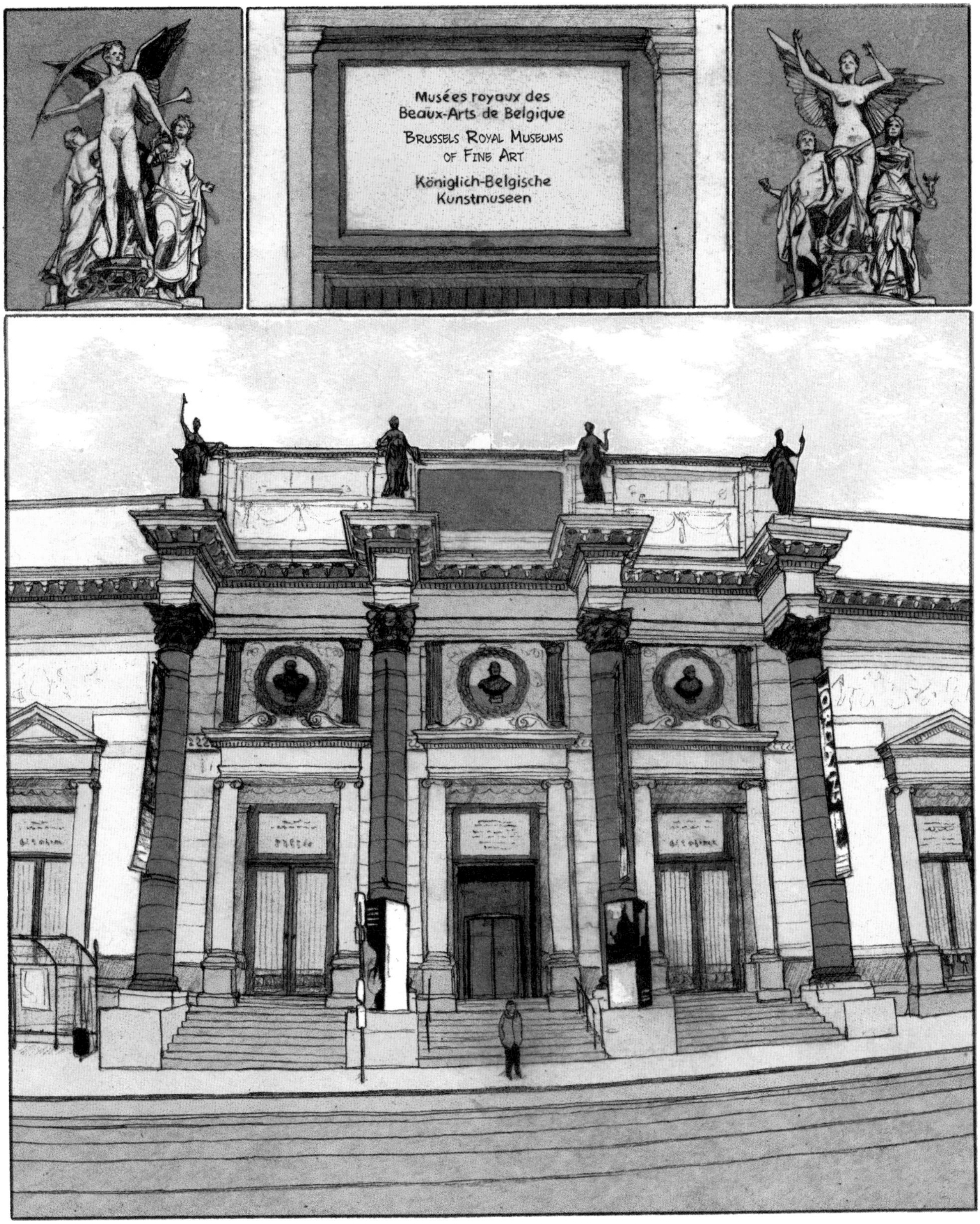
Musées royaux des
Beaux-Arts de Belgique
Brussels Royal Museums
of Fine Art
Königlich-Belgische
Kunstmuseen

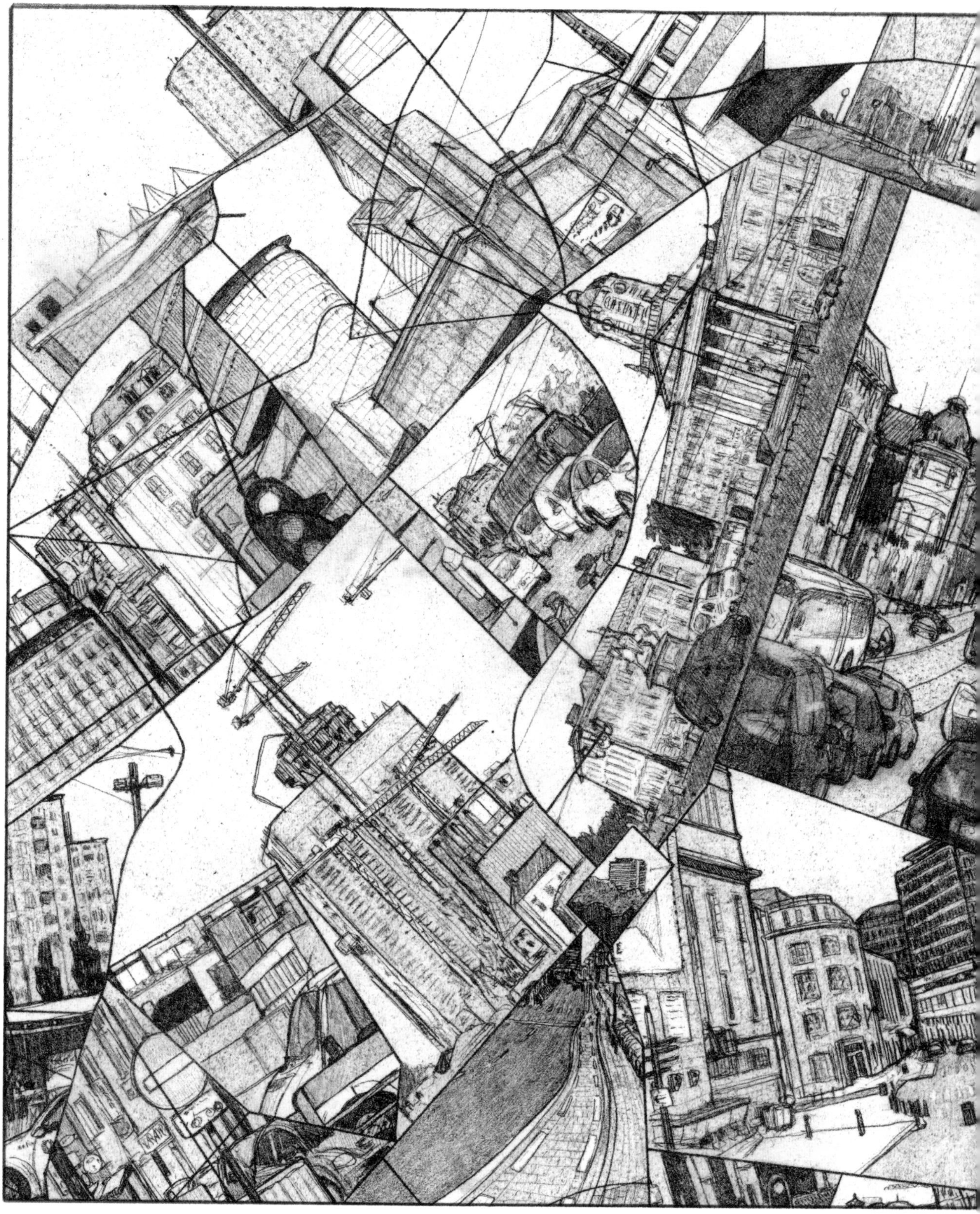

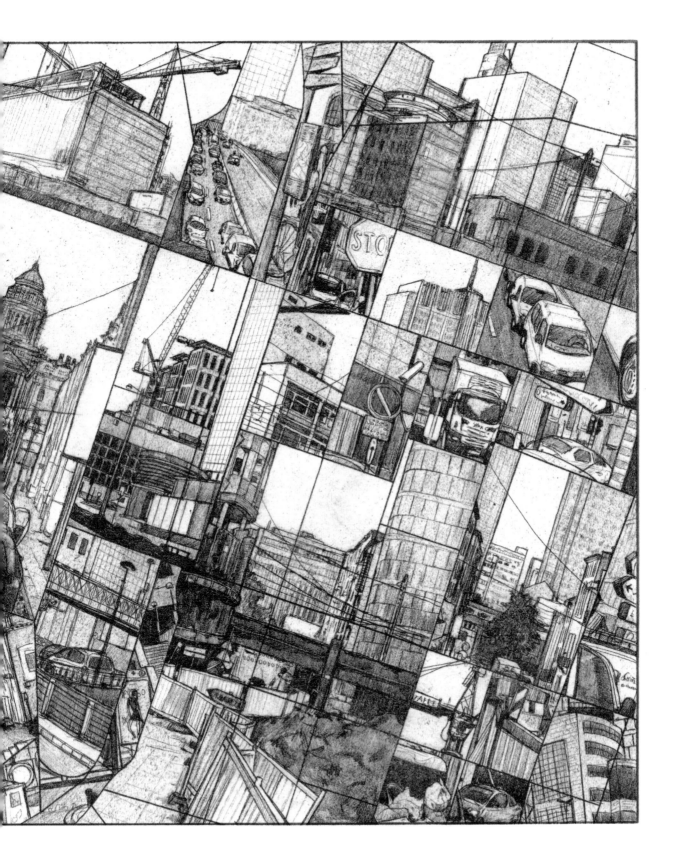

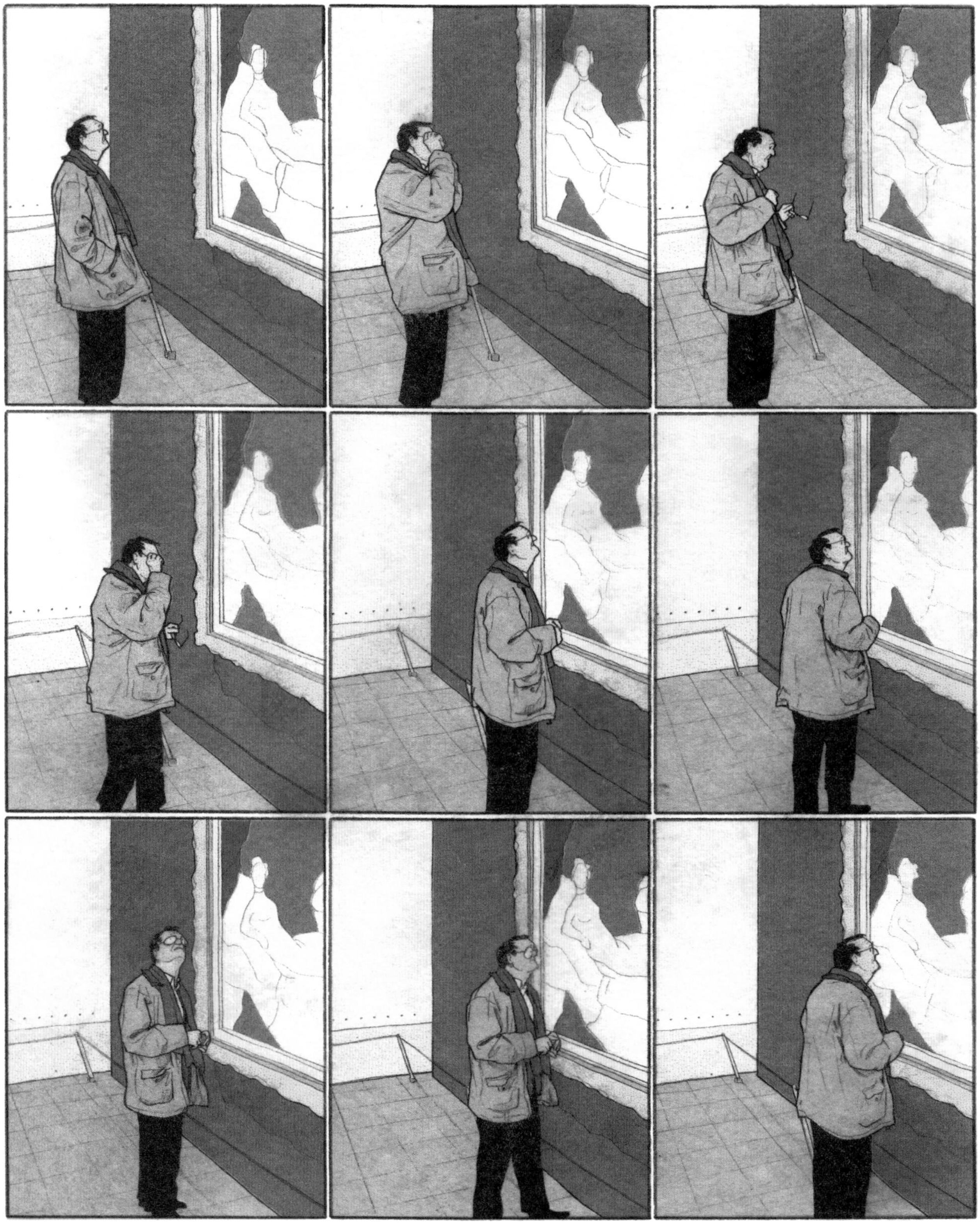

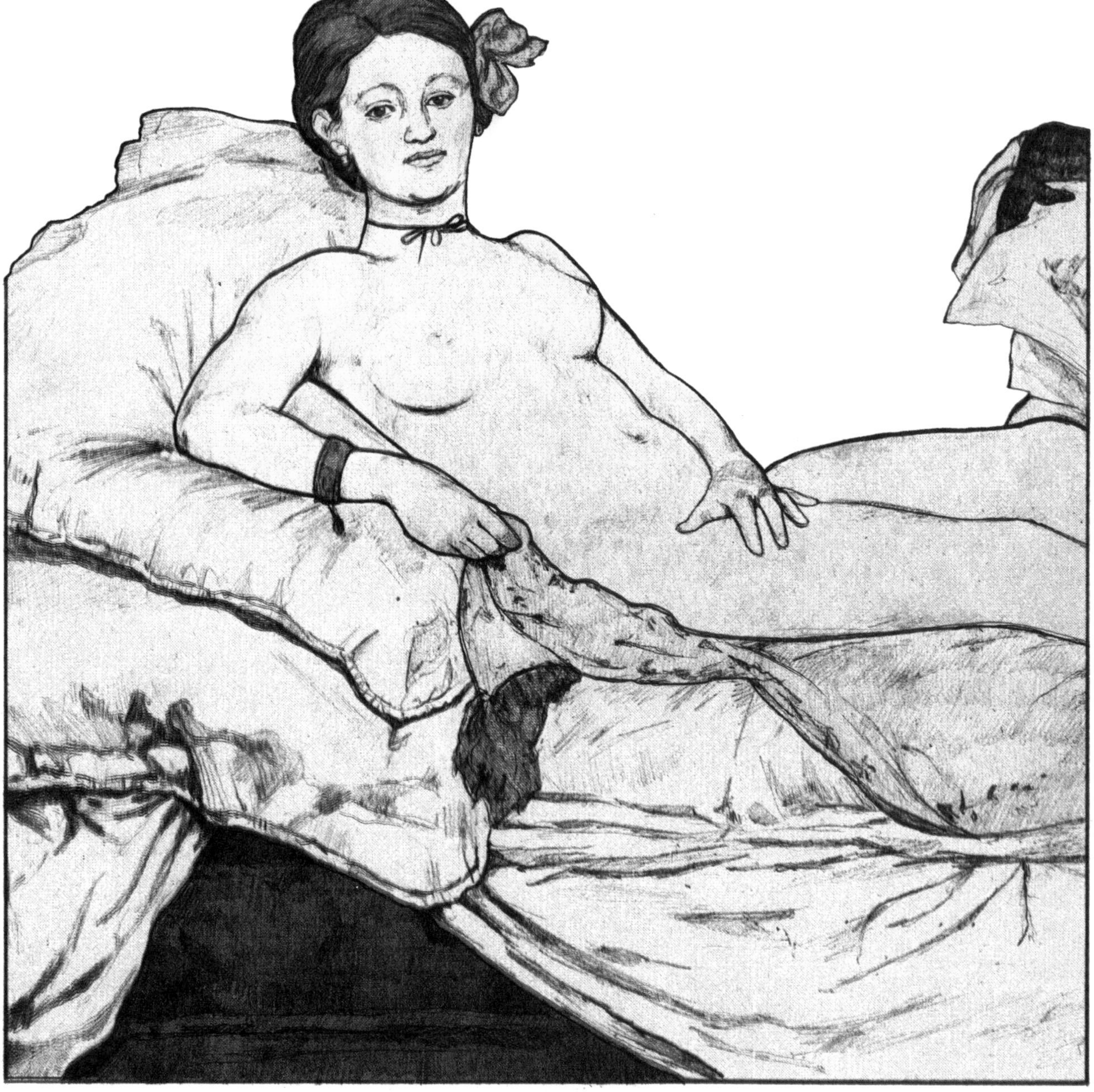

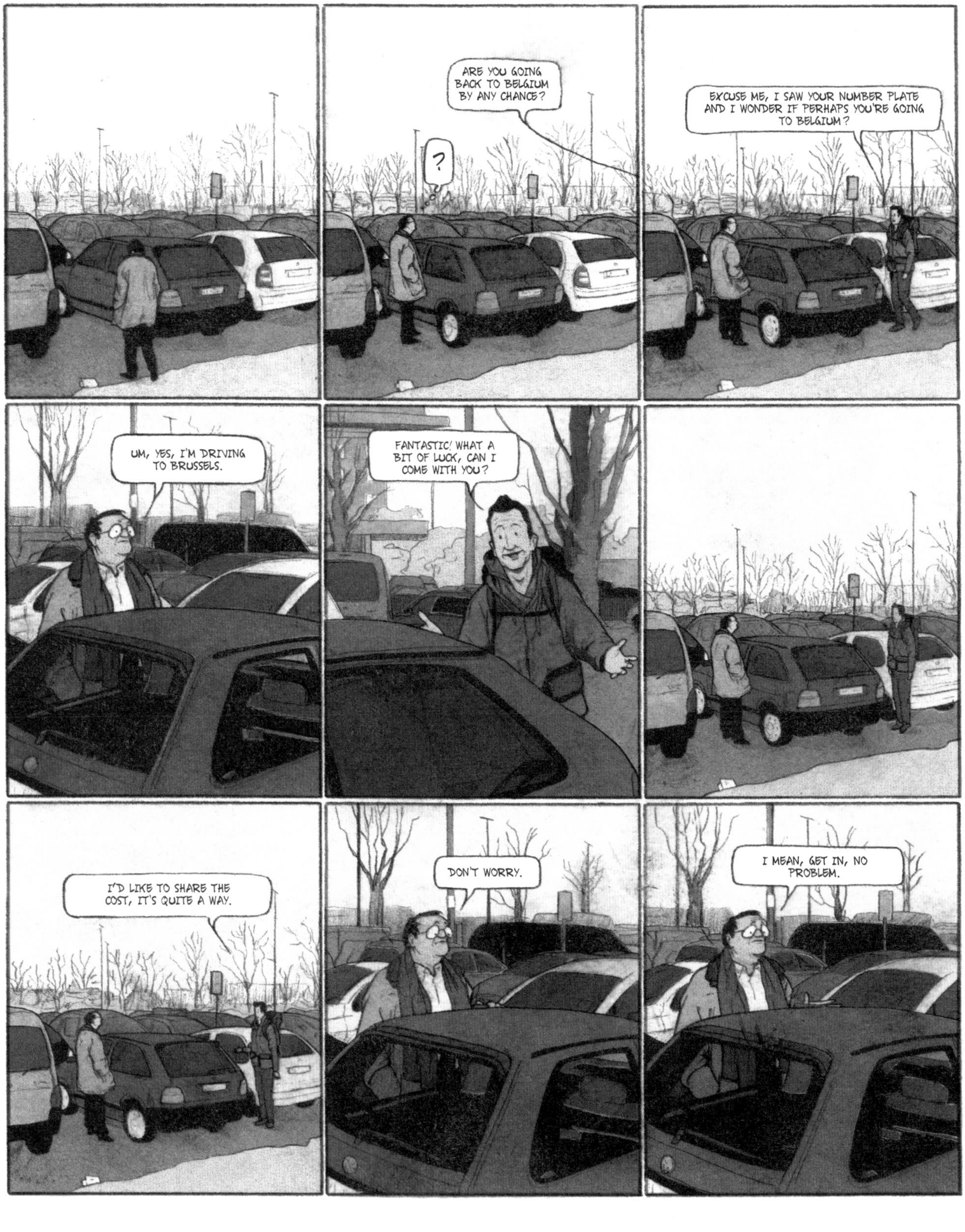
?
ARE YOU GOING BACK TO BELGIUM BY ANY CHANCE?
EXCUSE ME, I SAW YOUR NUMBER PLATE AND I WONDER IF PERHAPS YOU'RE GOING TO BELGIUM?
UM, YES, I'M DRIVING TO BRUSSELS.
FANTASTIC! WHAT A BIT OF LUCK, CAN I COME WITH YOU?
I'D LIKE TO SHARE THE COST, IT'S QUITE A WAY.
DON'T WORRY.
I MEAN, GET IN, NO PROBLEM.

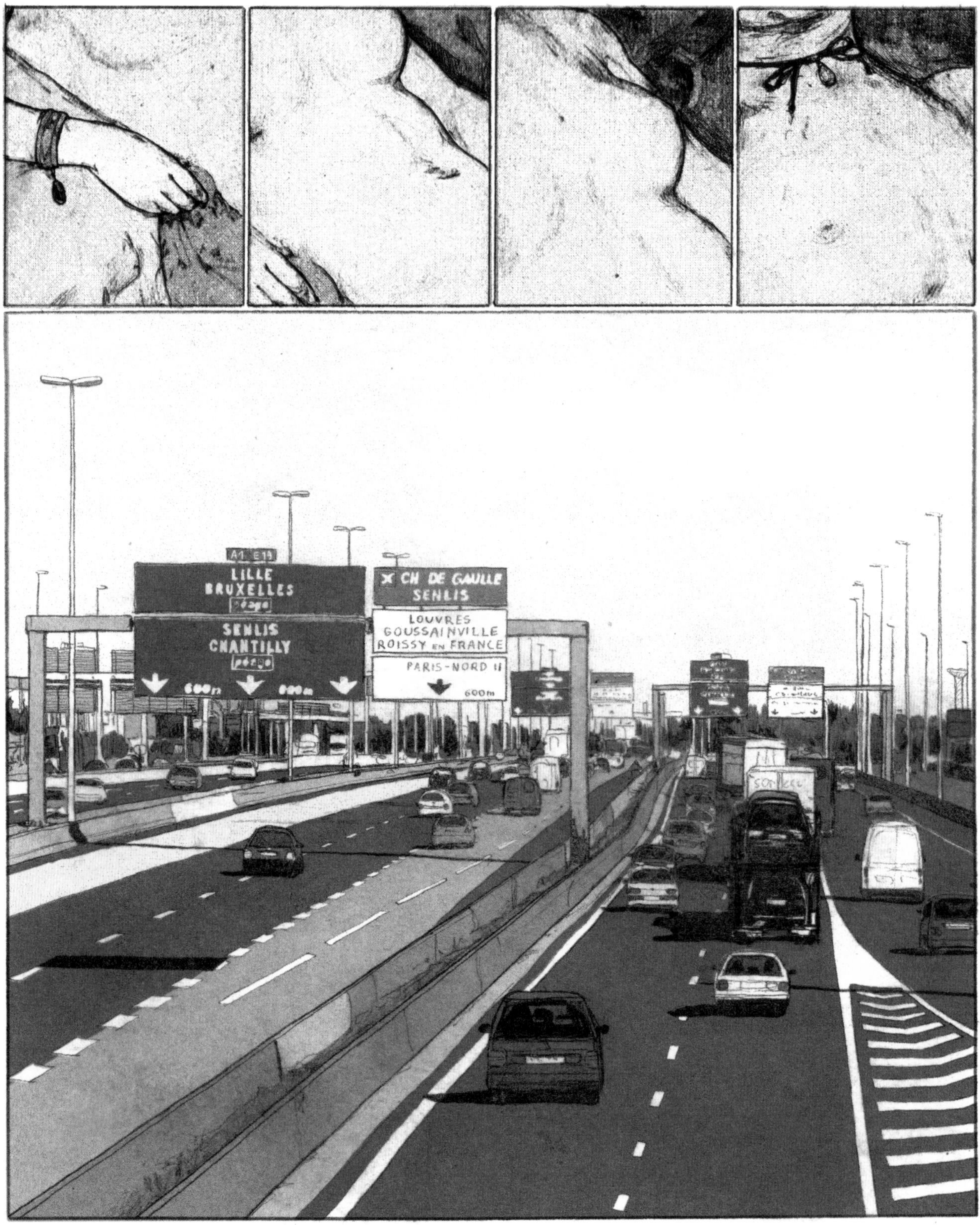

A1 E19
LILLE
BRUXELLES
SENLIS
CHANTILLY
CH DE GAULLE
SENLIS
LOUVRES
GOUSSAINVILLE
ROISSY EN FRANCE
PARIS-NORD II
600m

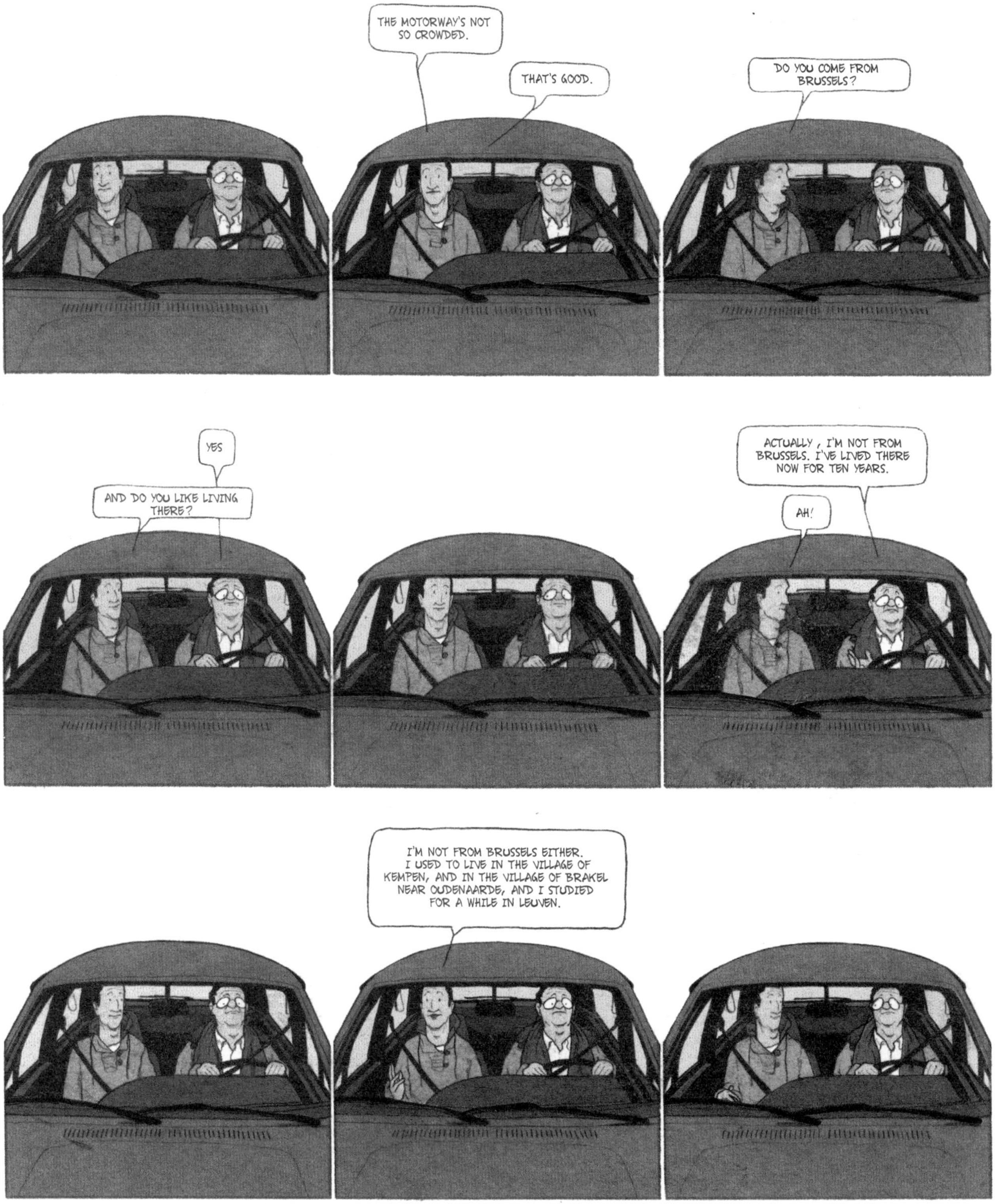
THE MOTORWAY'S NOT SO CROWDED.
THAT'S GOOD.
DO YOU COME FROM BRUSSELS?
YES
AND DO YOU LIKE LIVING THERE?
ACTUALLY, I'M NOT FROM BRUSSELS. I'VE LIVED THERE NOW FOR TEN YEARS.
AH!
I'M NOT FROM BRUSSELS EITHER. I USED TO LIVE IN THE VILLAGE OF KEMPEN, AND IN THE VILLAGE OF BRAKEL NEAR OUDENAARDE, AND I STUDIED FOR A WHILE IN LEUVEN.

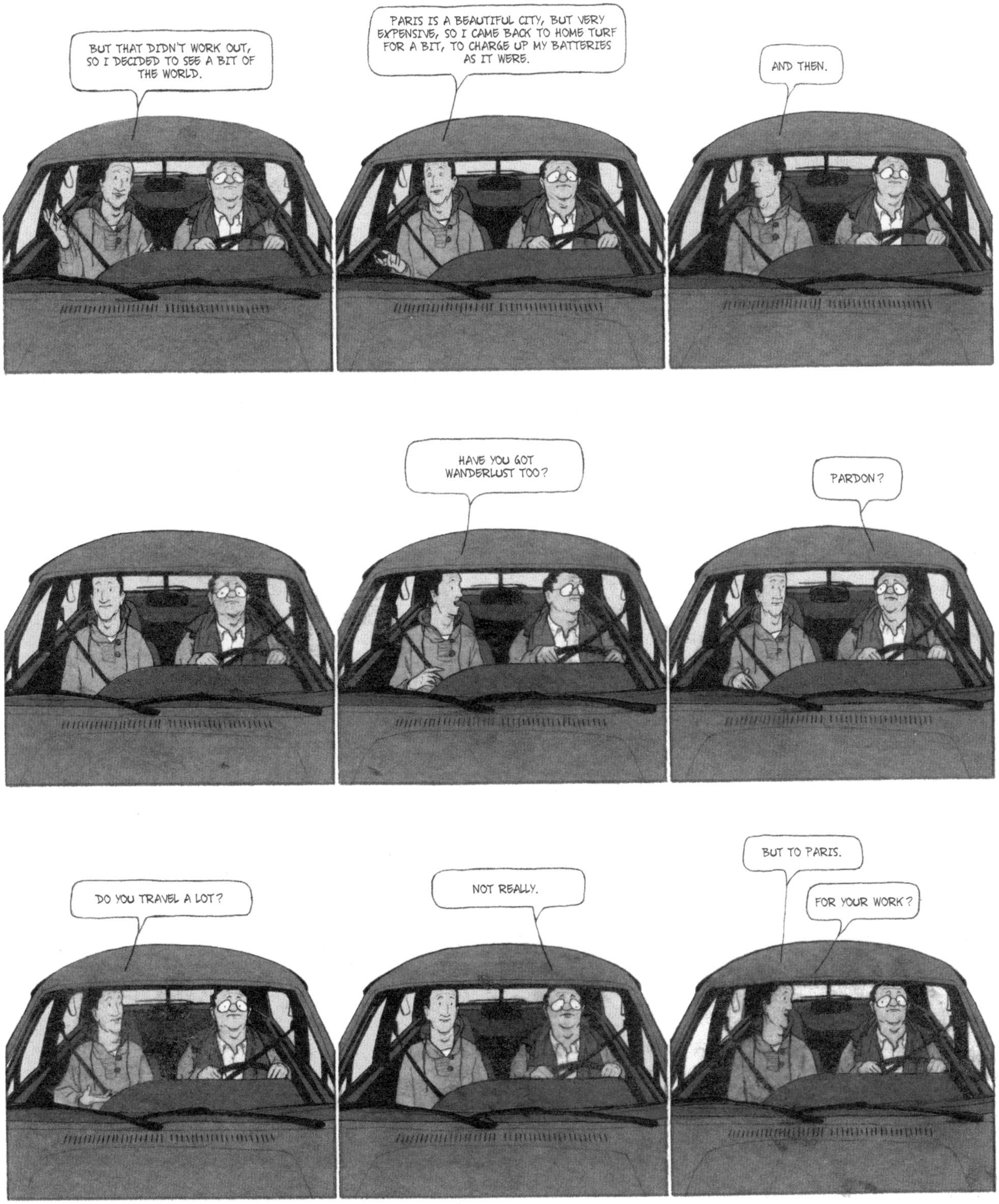

BUT THAT DIDN'T WORK OUT, SO I DECIDED TO SEE A BIT OF THE WORLD.
PARIS IS A BEAUTIFUL CITY, BUT VERY EXPENSIVE, SO I CAME BACK TO HOME TURF FOR A BIT, TO CHARGE UP MY BATTERIES AS IT WERE.
AND THEN.
HAVE YOU GOT WANDERLUST TOO?
PARDON?
DO YOU TRAVEL A LOT?
NOT REALLY.
BUT TO PARIS.
FOR YOUR WORK?

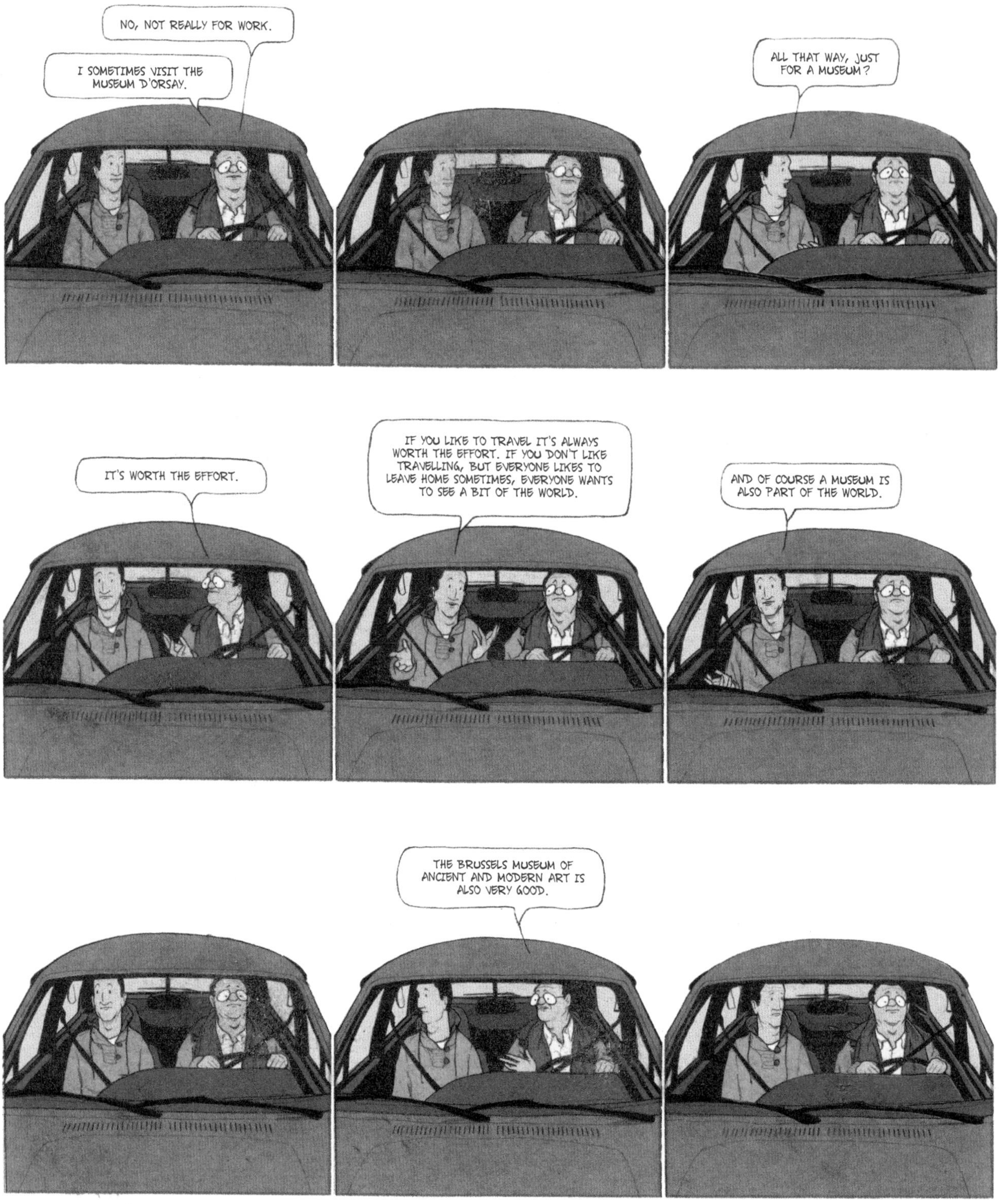
I SOMETIMES VISIT THE MUSEUM D'ORSAY.
NO, NOT REALLY FOR WORK.
ALL THAT WAY, JUST FOR A MUSEUM?
IT'S WORTH THE EFFORT.
IF YOU LIKE TO TRAVEL IT'S ALWAYS WORTH THE EFFORT. IF YOU DON'T LIKE TRAVELLING, BUT EVERYONE LIKES TO LEAVE HOME SOMETIMES, EVERYONE WANTS TO SEE A BIT OF THE WORLD.
AND OF COURSE A MUSEUM IS ALSO PART OF THE WORLD.
THE BRUSSELS MUSEUM OF ANCIENT AND MODERN ART IS ALSO VERY GOOD.

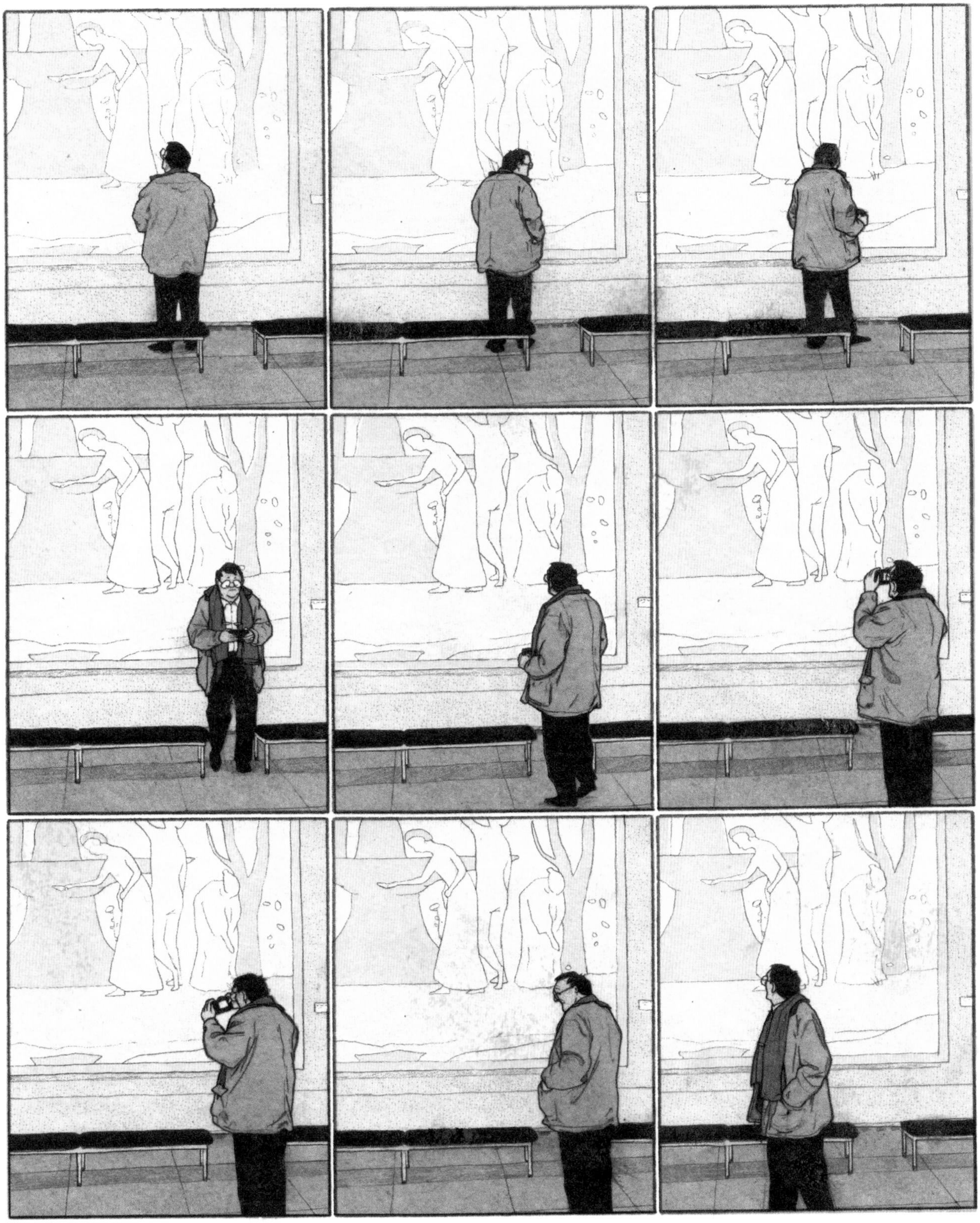

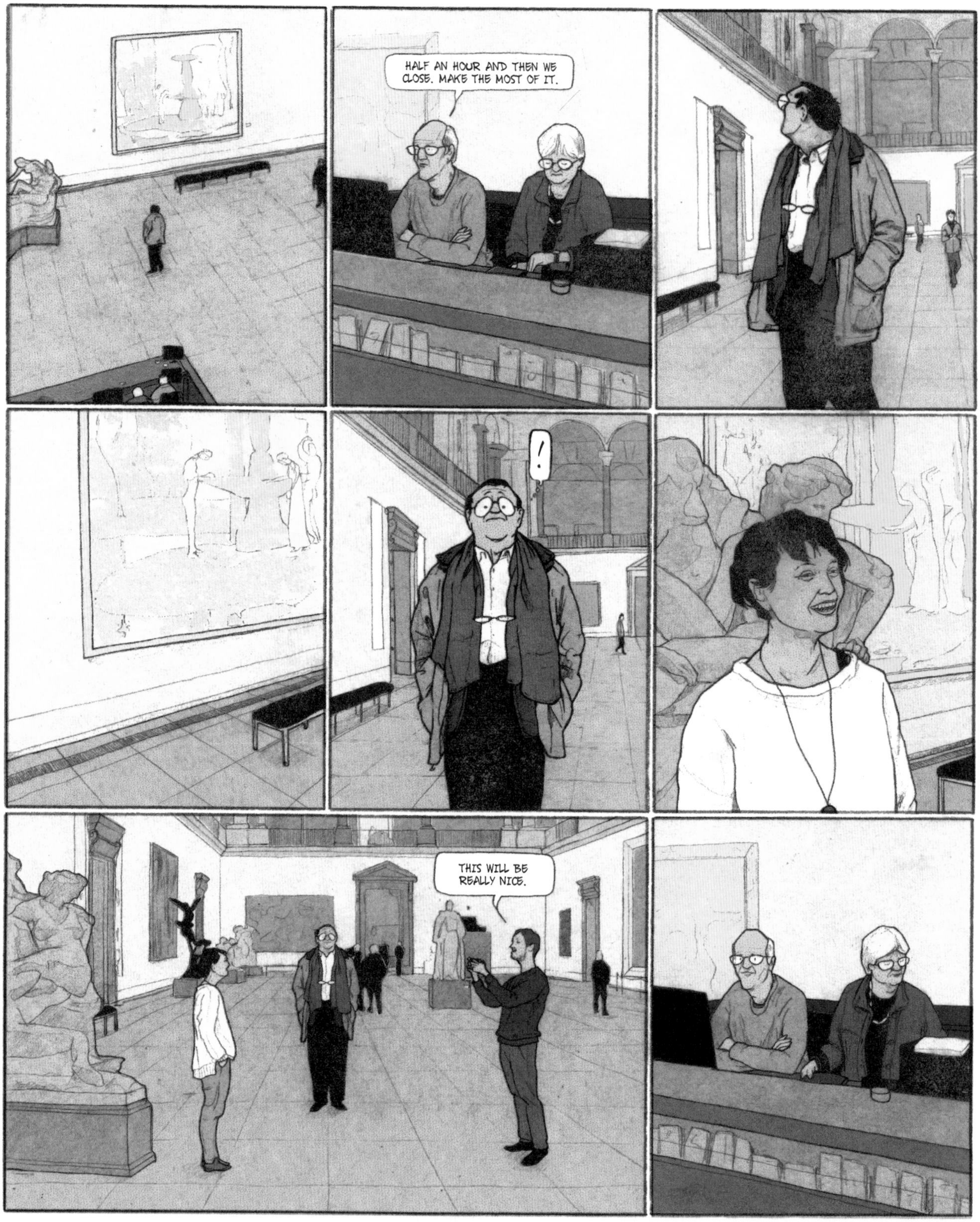
HALF AN HOUR AND THEN WE CLOSE. MAKE THE MOST OF IT.
!
THIS WILL BE REALLY NICE.

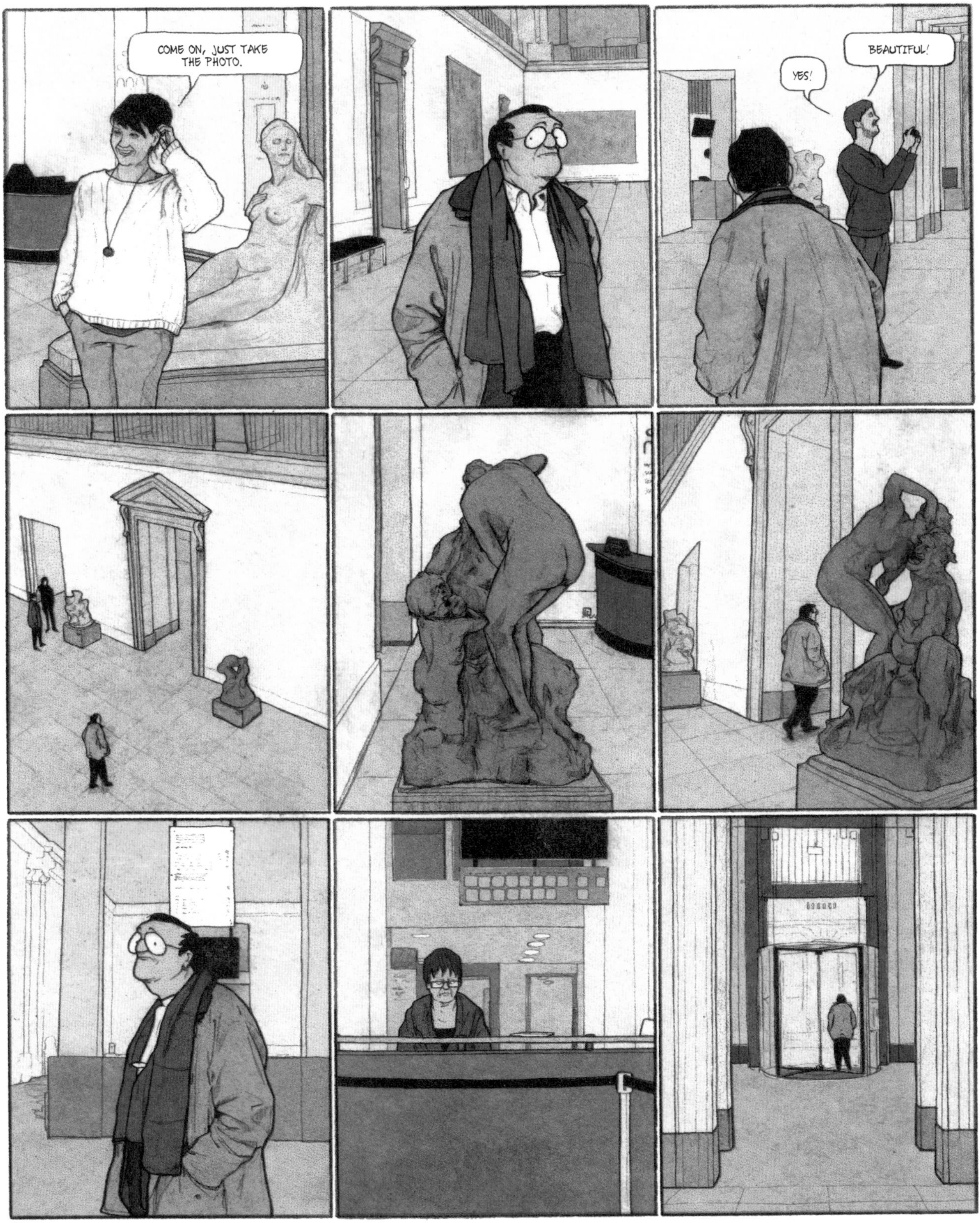
COME ON, JUST TAKE THE PHOTO.
YES!
BEAUTIFUL!

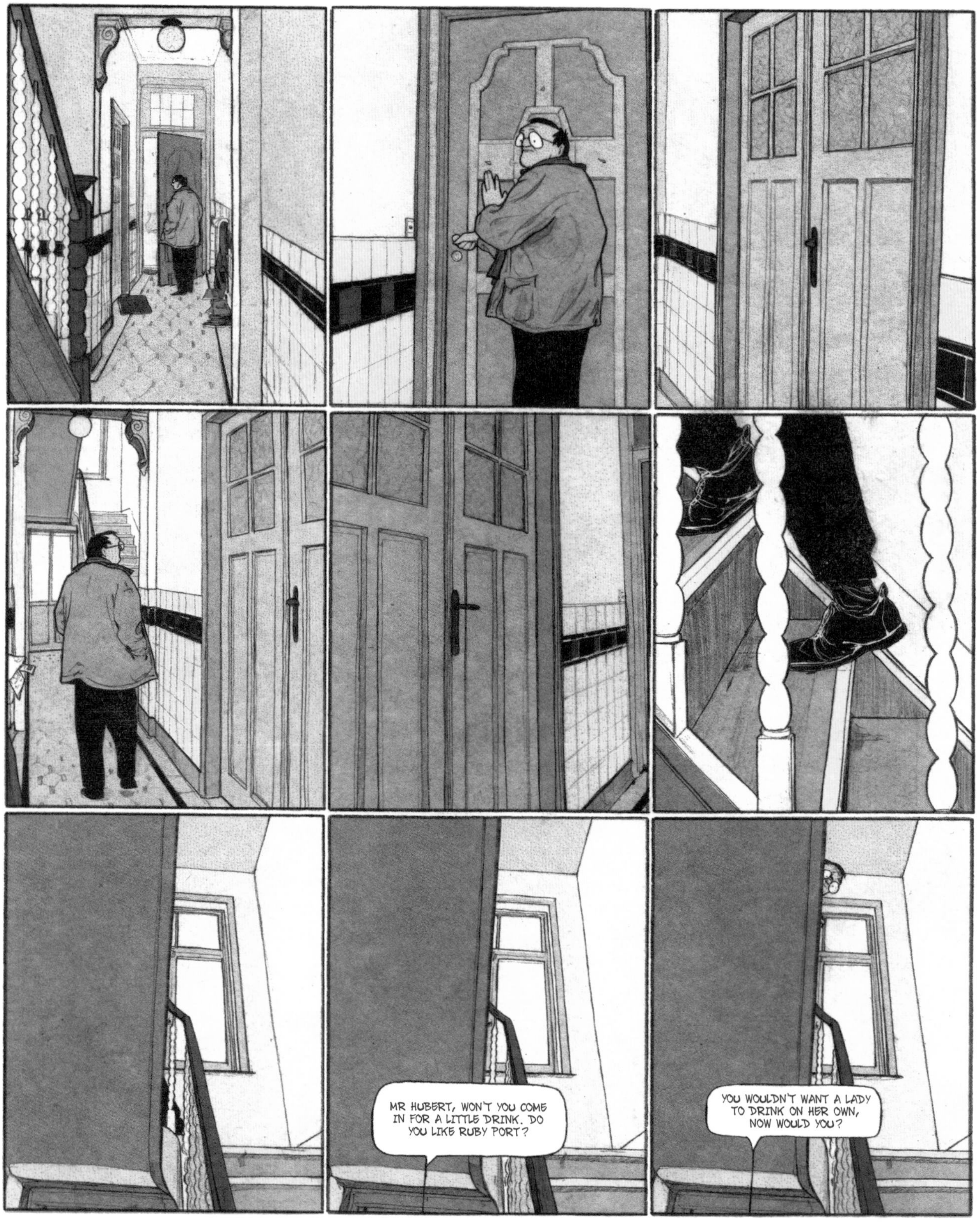
MR HUBERT, WON'T YOU COME IN FOR A LITTLE DRINK. DO YOU LIKE RUBY PORT?
YOU WOULDN'T WANT A LADY TO DRINK ON HER OWN, NOW WOULD YOU?

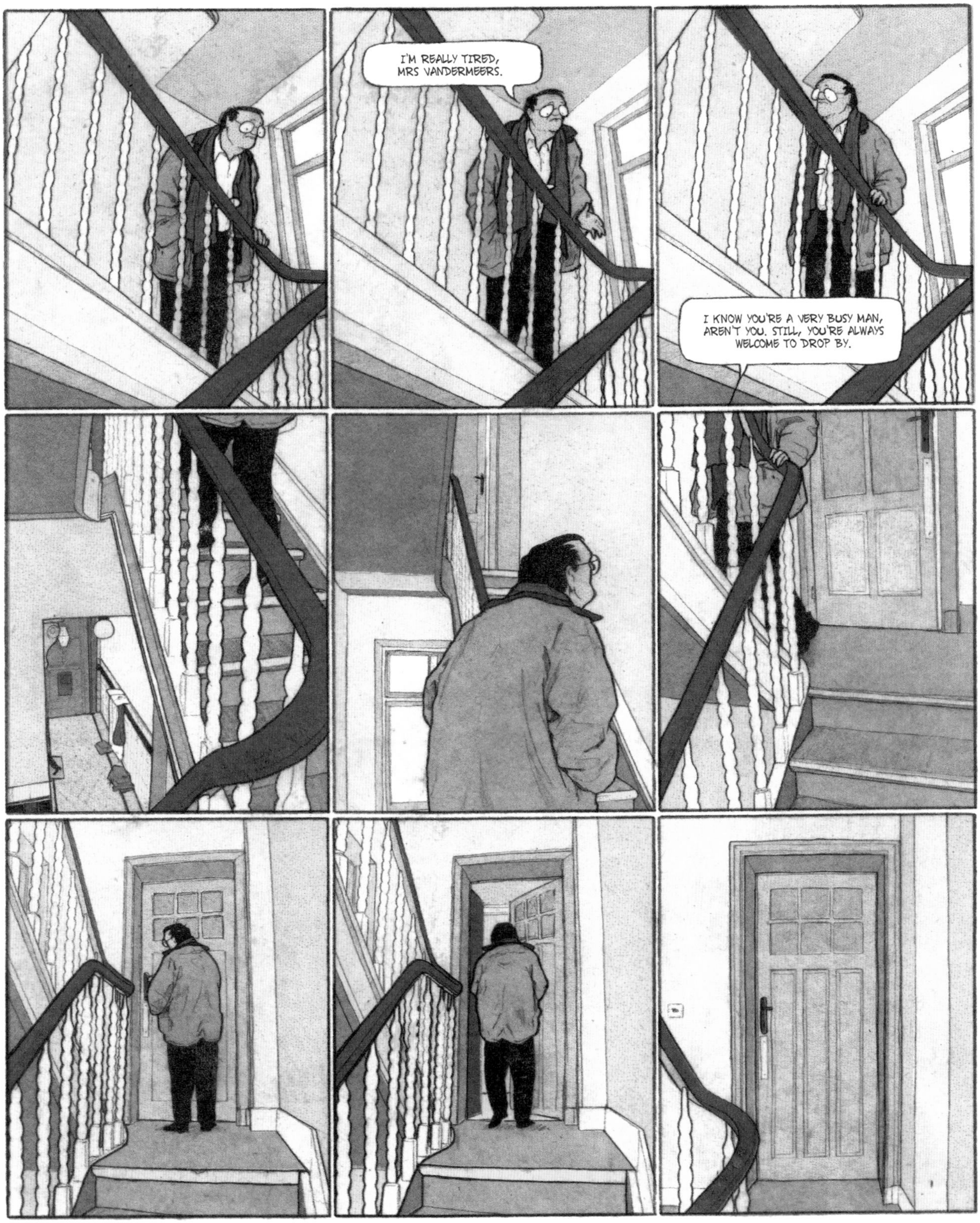
I'M REALLY TIRED, MRS VANDERMEERS.
I KNOW YOU'RE A VERY BUSY MAN, AREN'T YOU. STILL, YOU'RE ALWAYS WELCOME TO DROP BY.

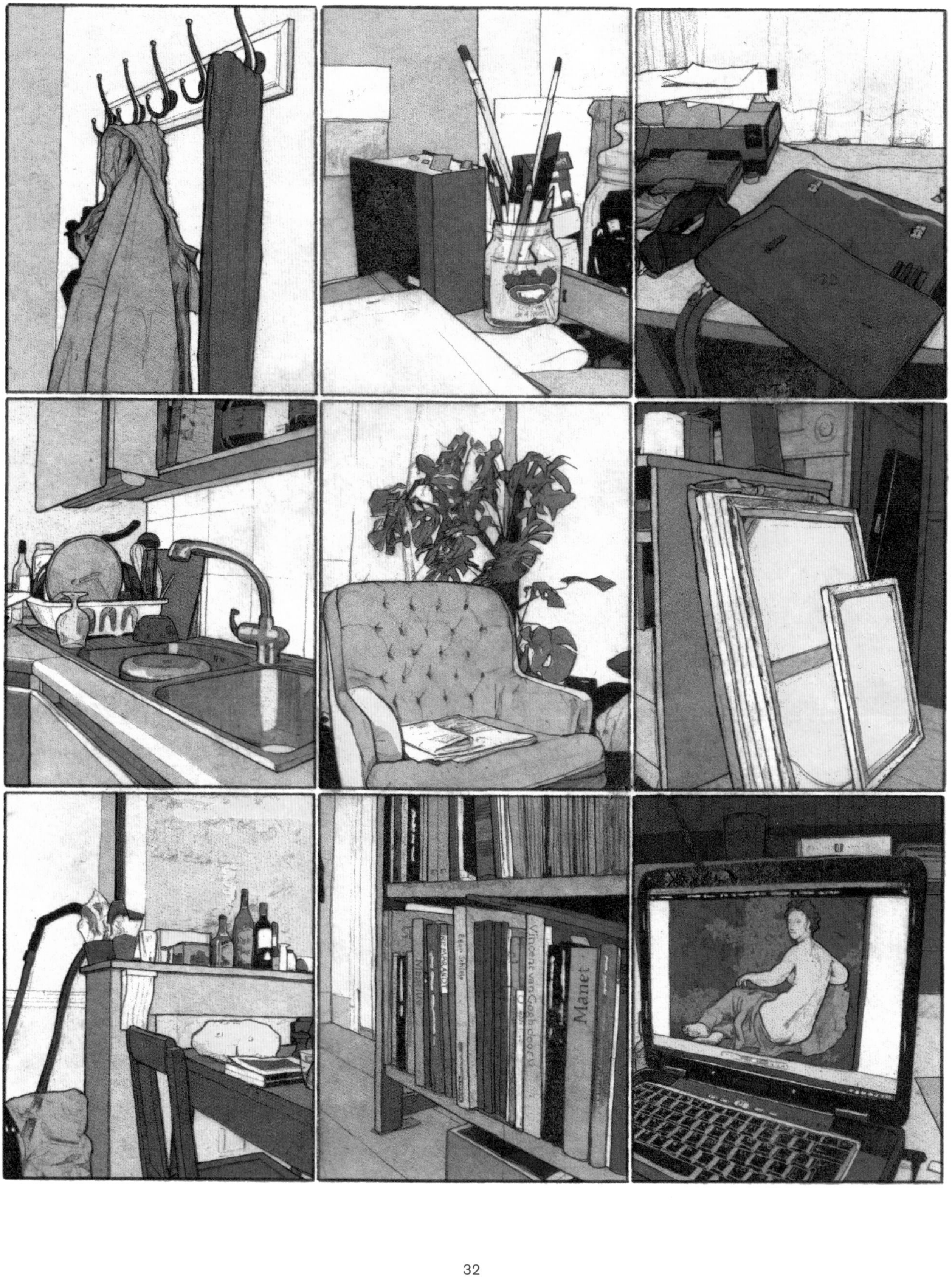

Matisse
REMBRANDT
Egon Schiele
Vincent van Gogh door V.
Manet

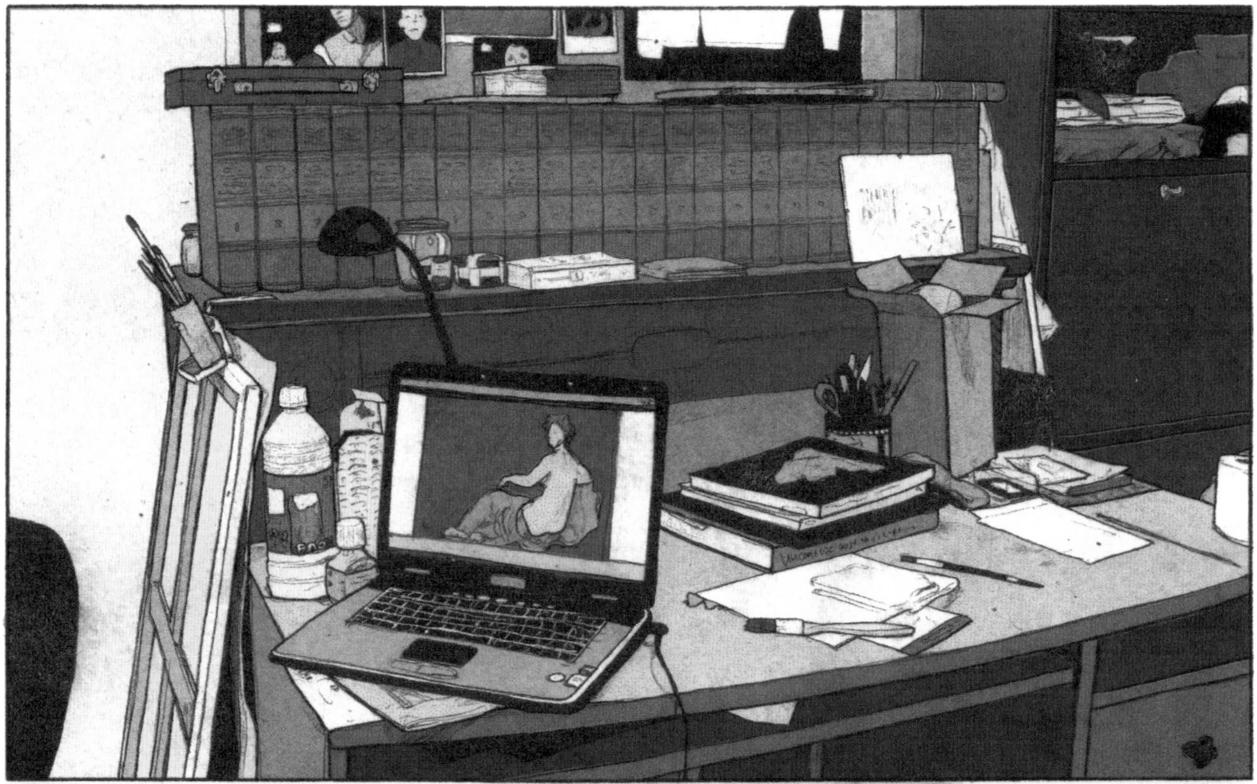

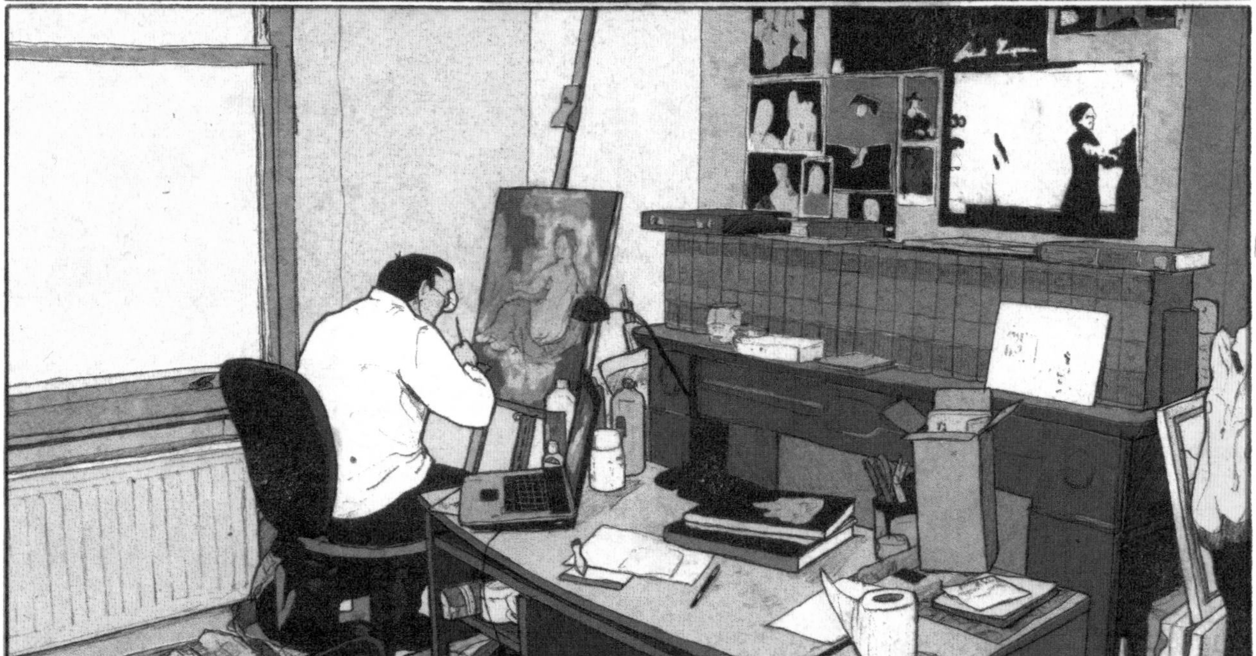

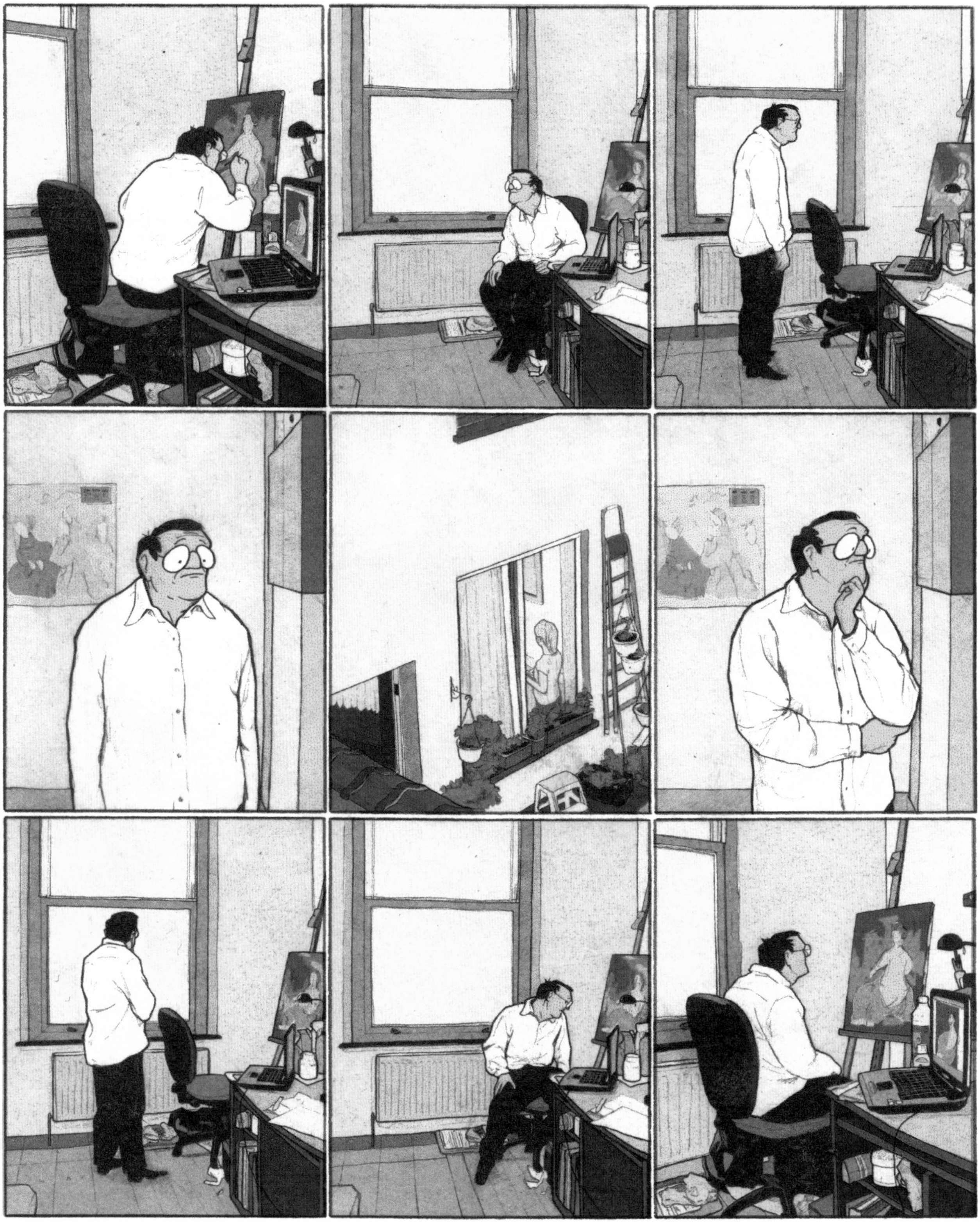

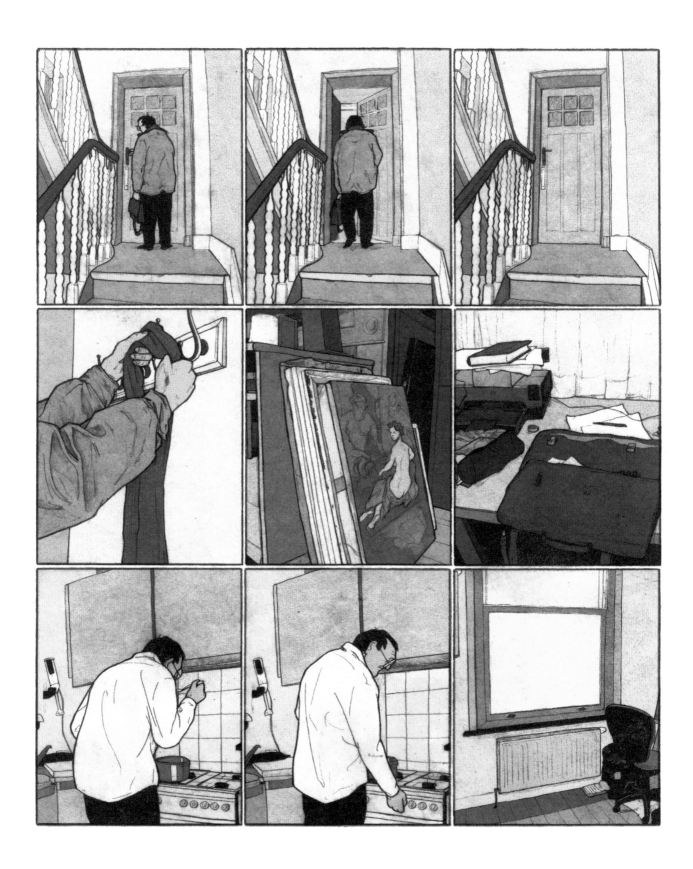

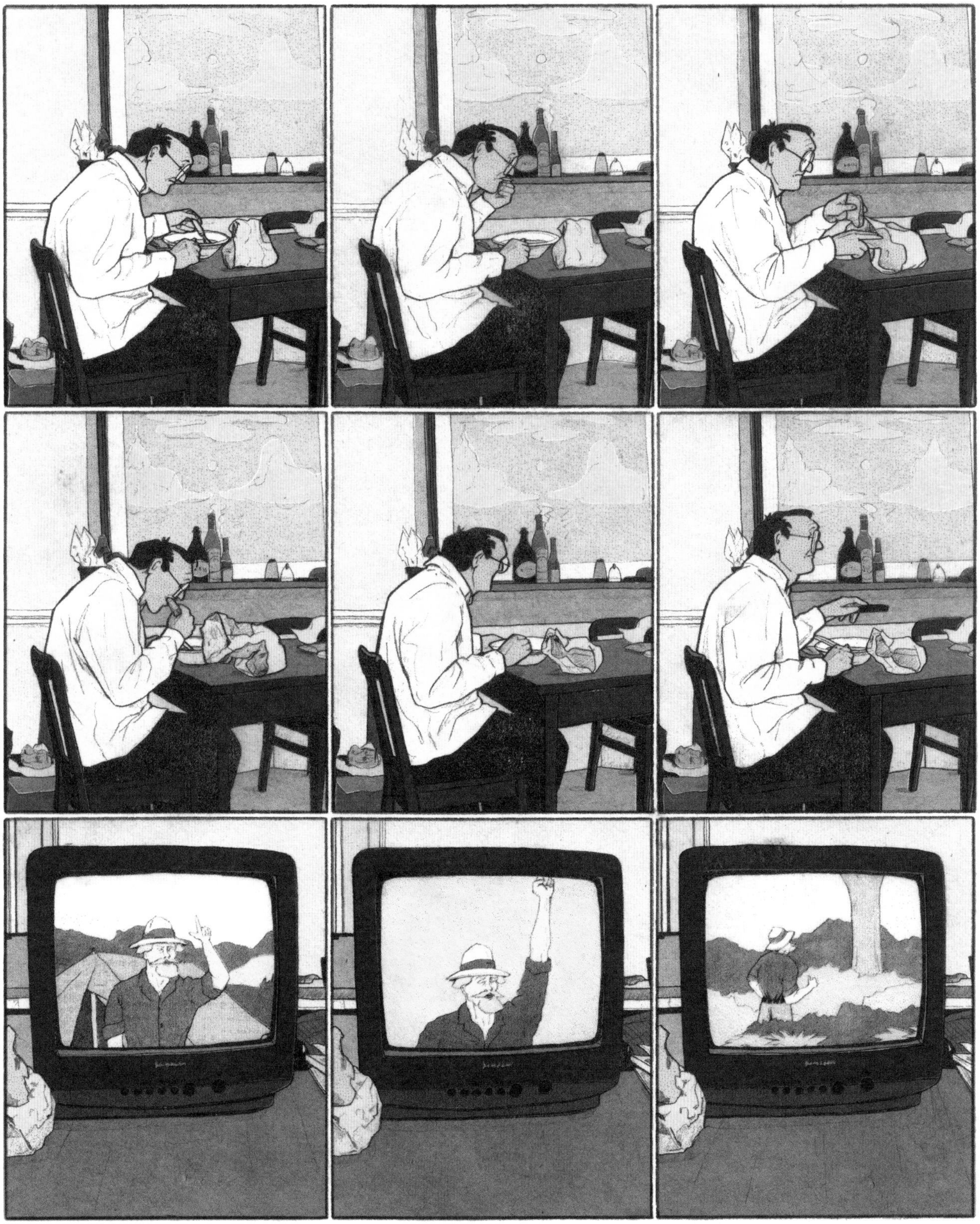

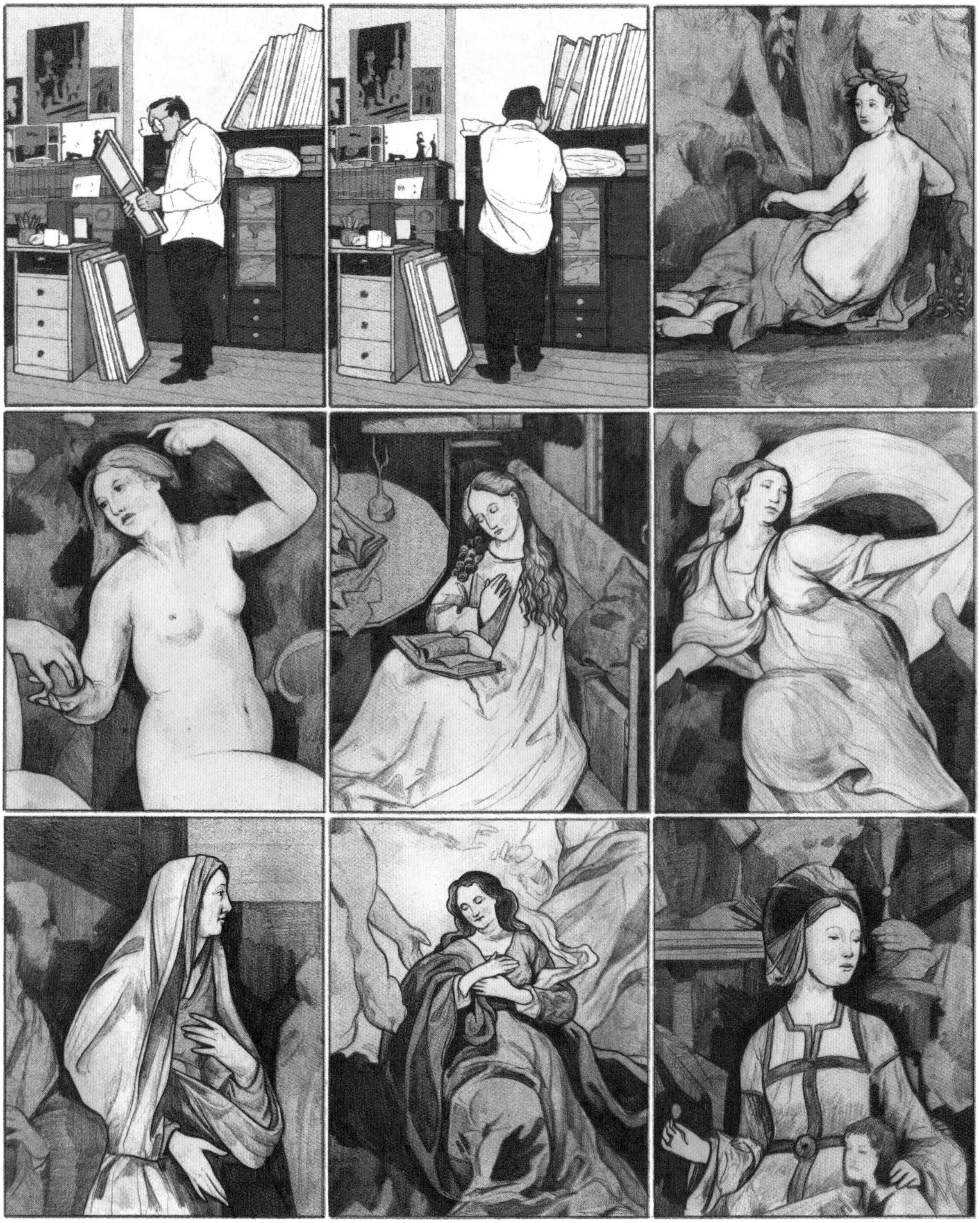

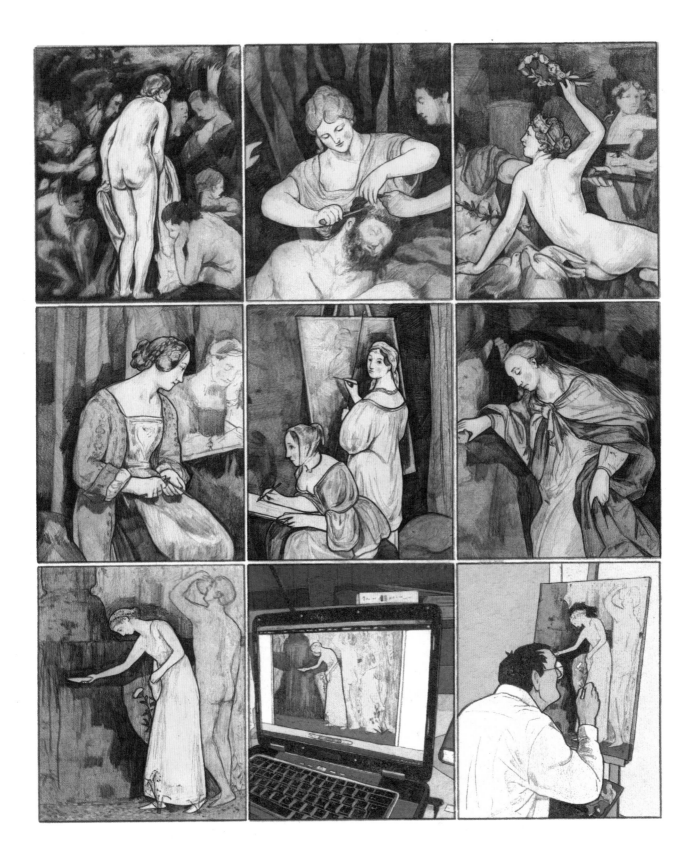

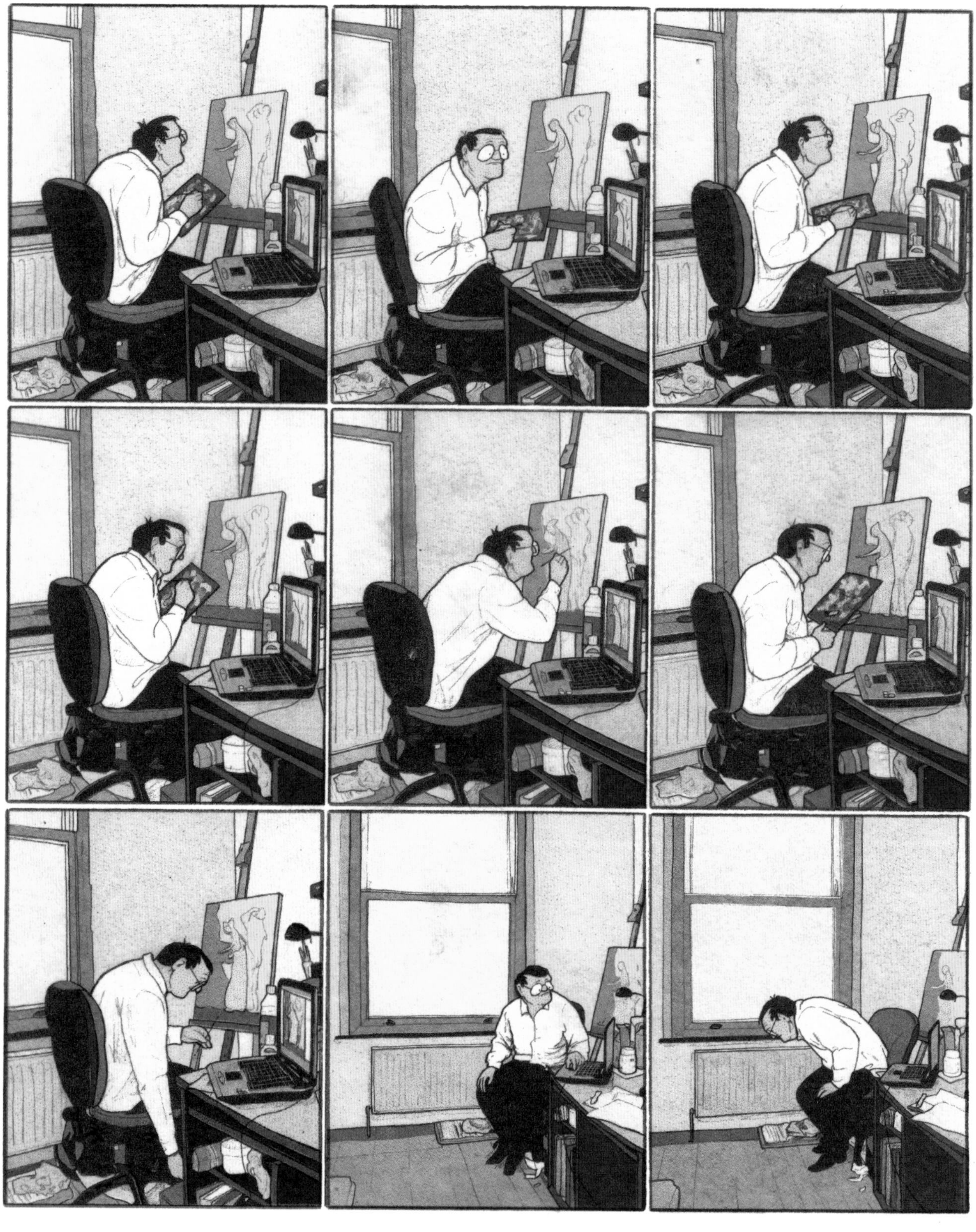

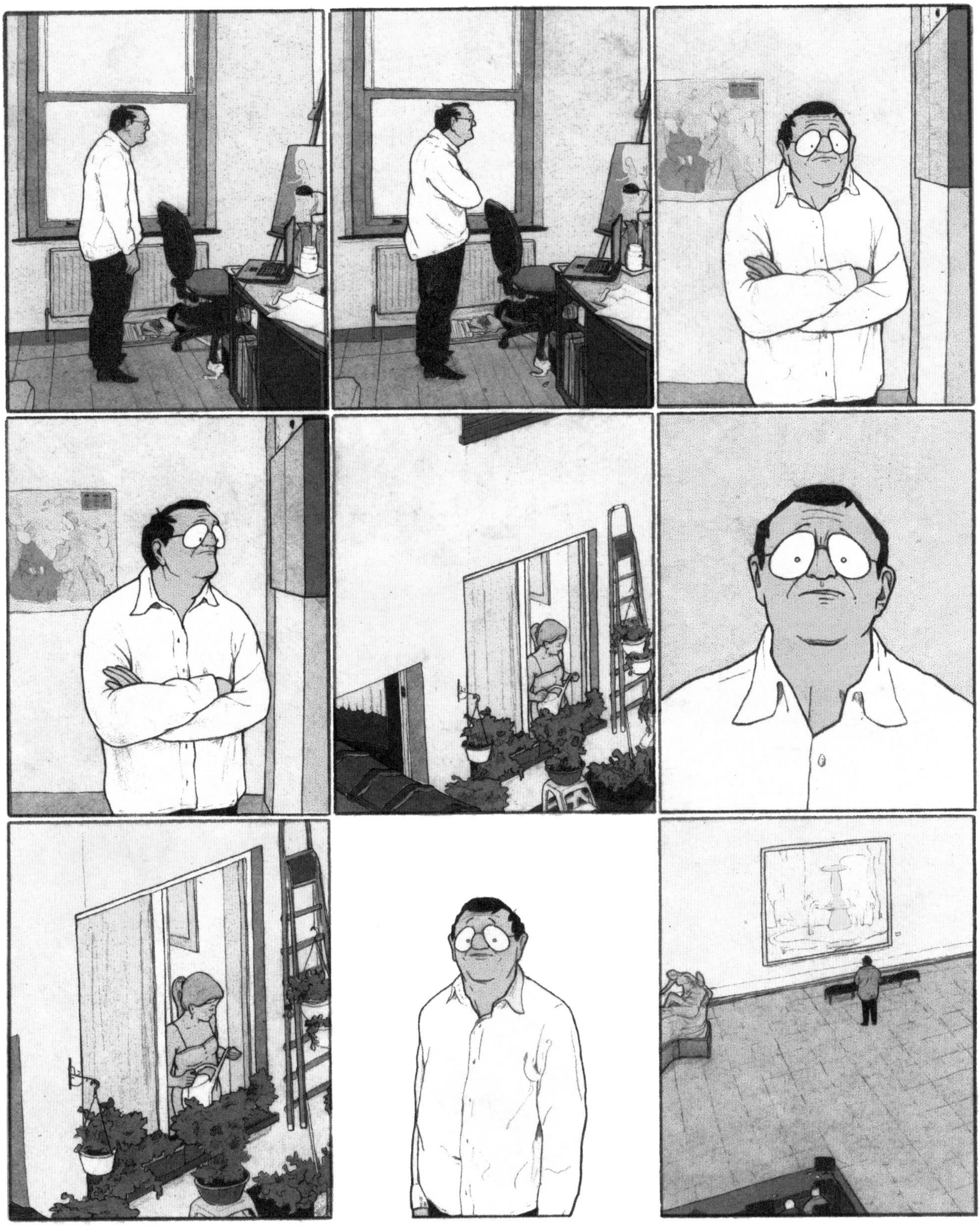

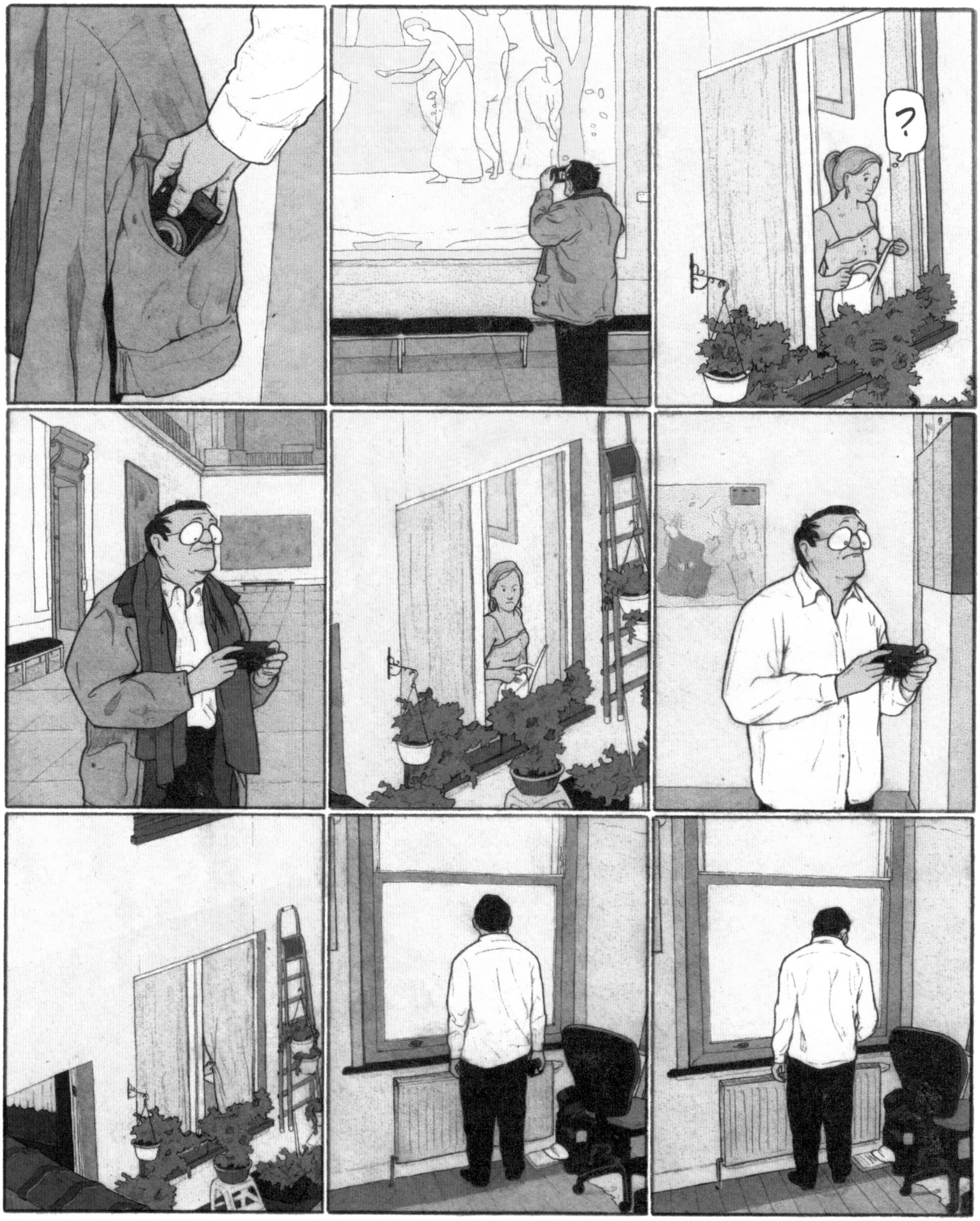
?

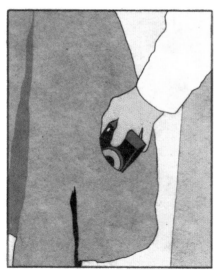

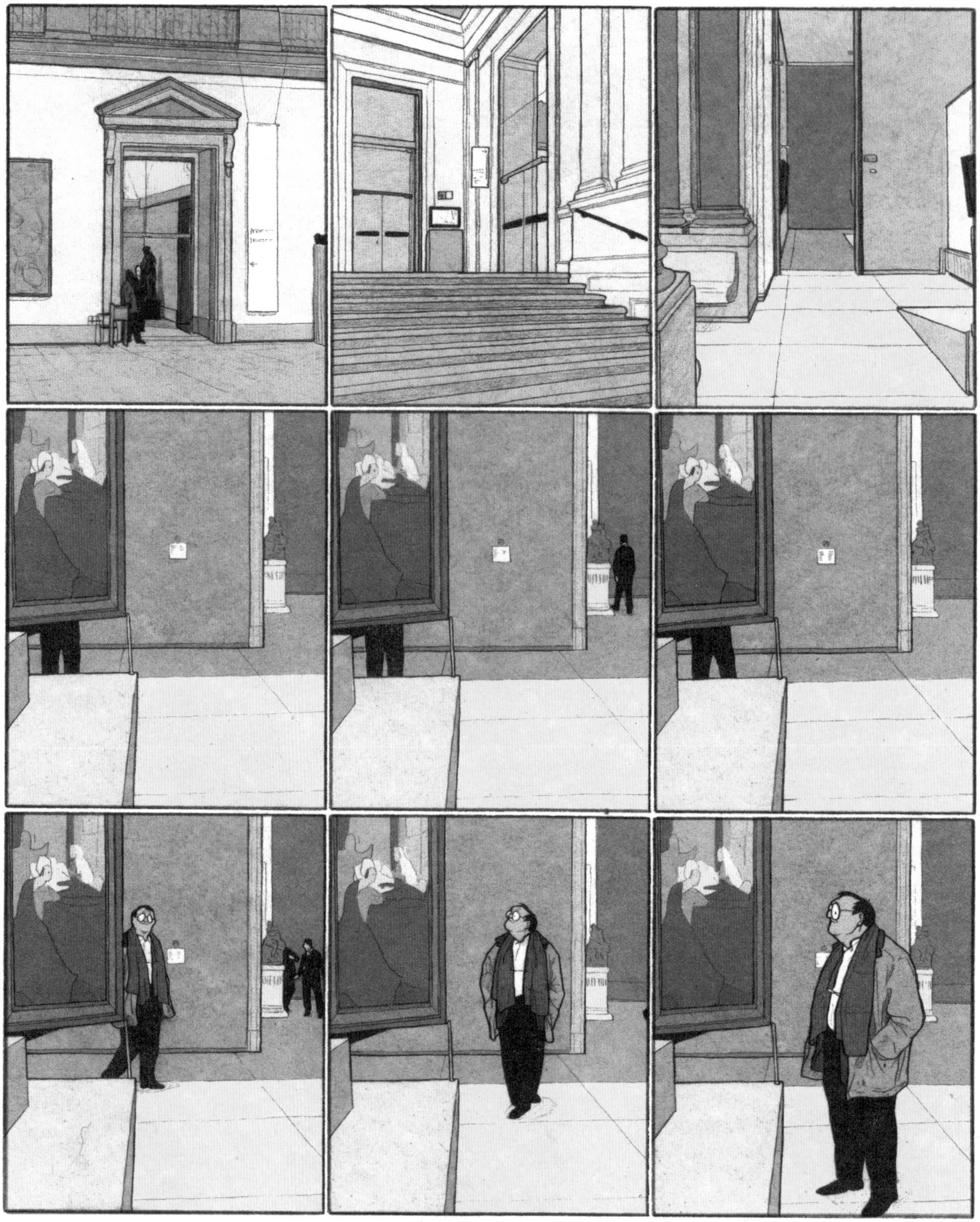

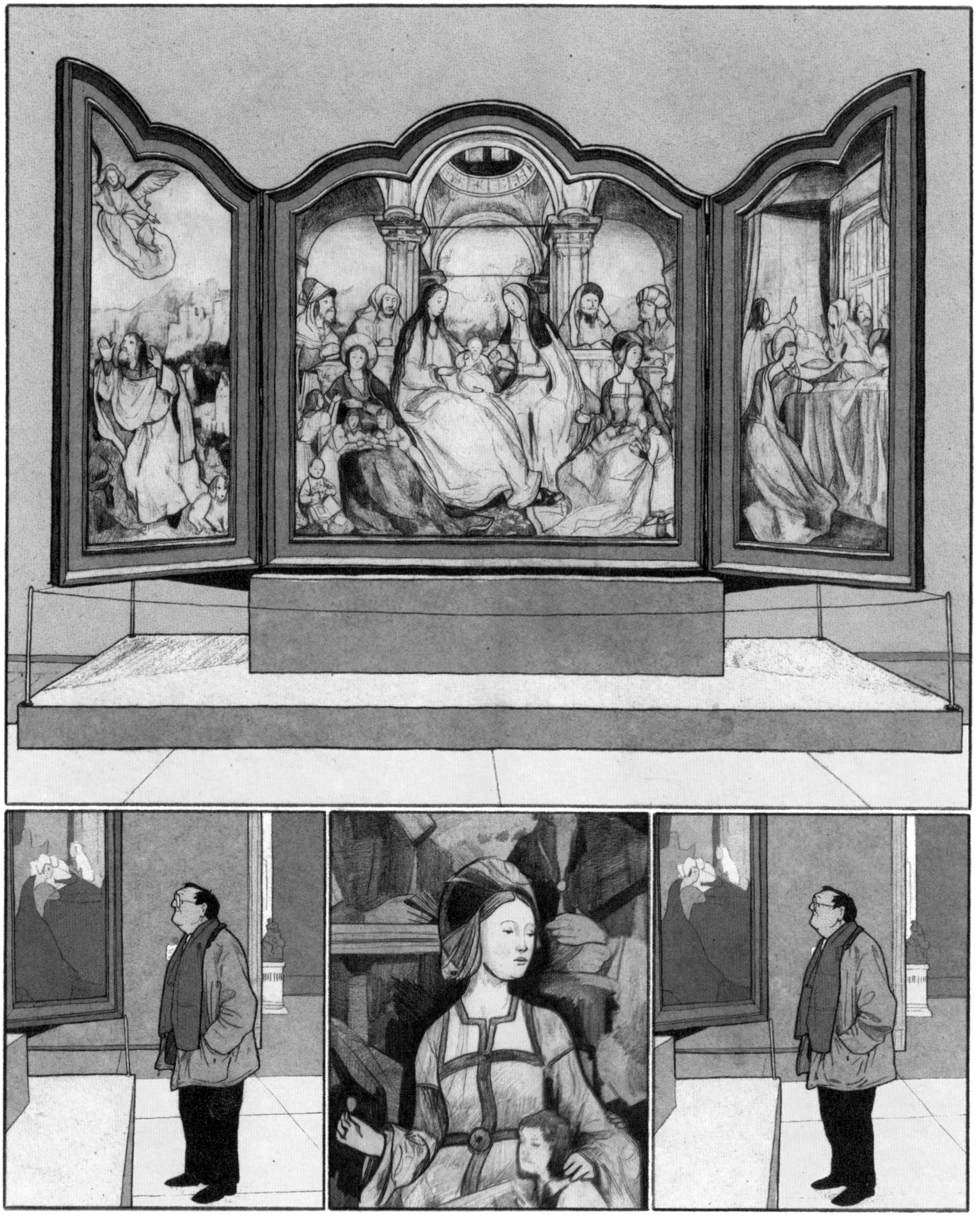

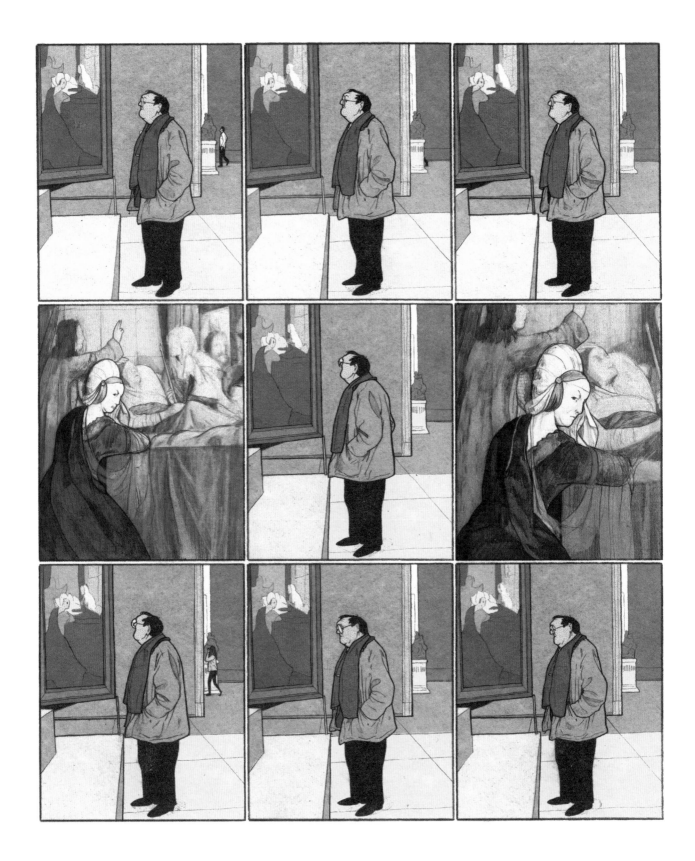

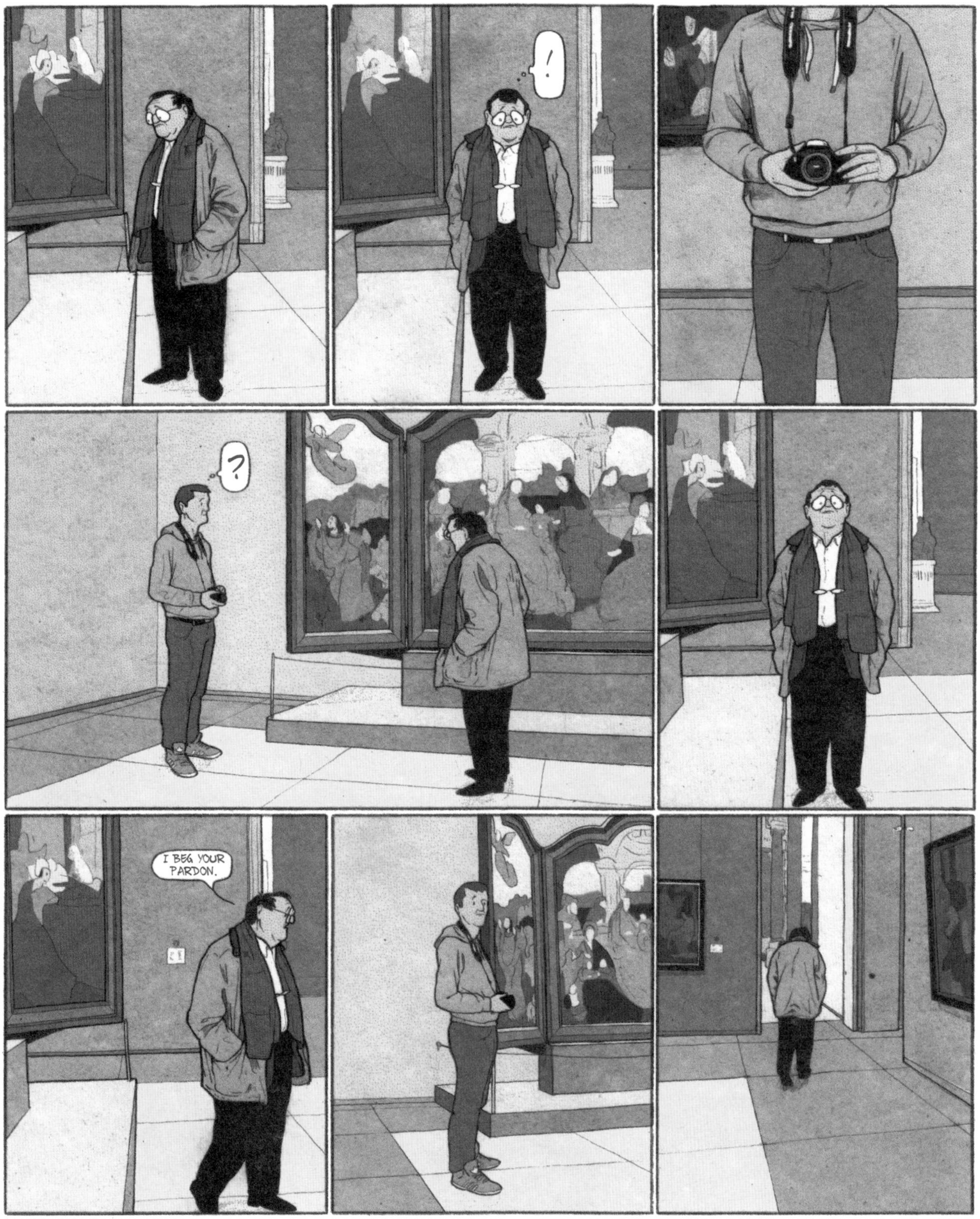
!
?
I BEG YOUR PARDON.

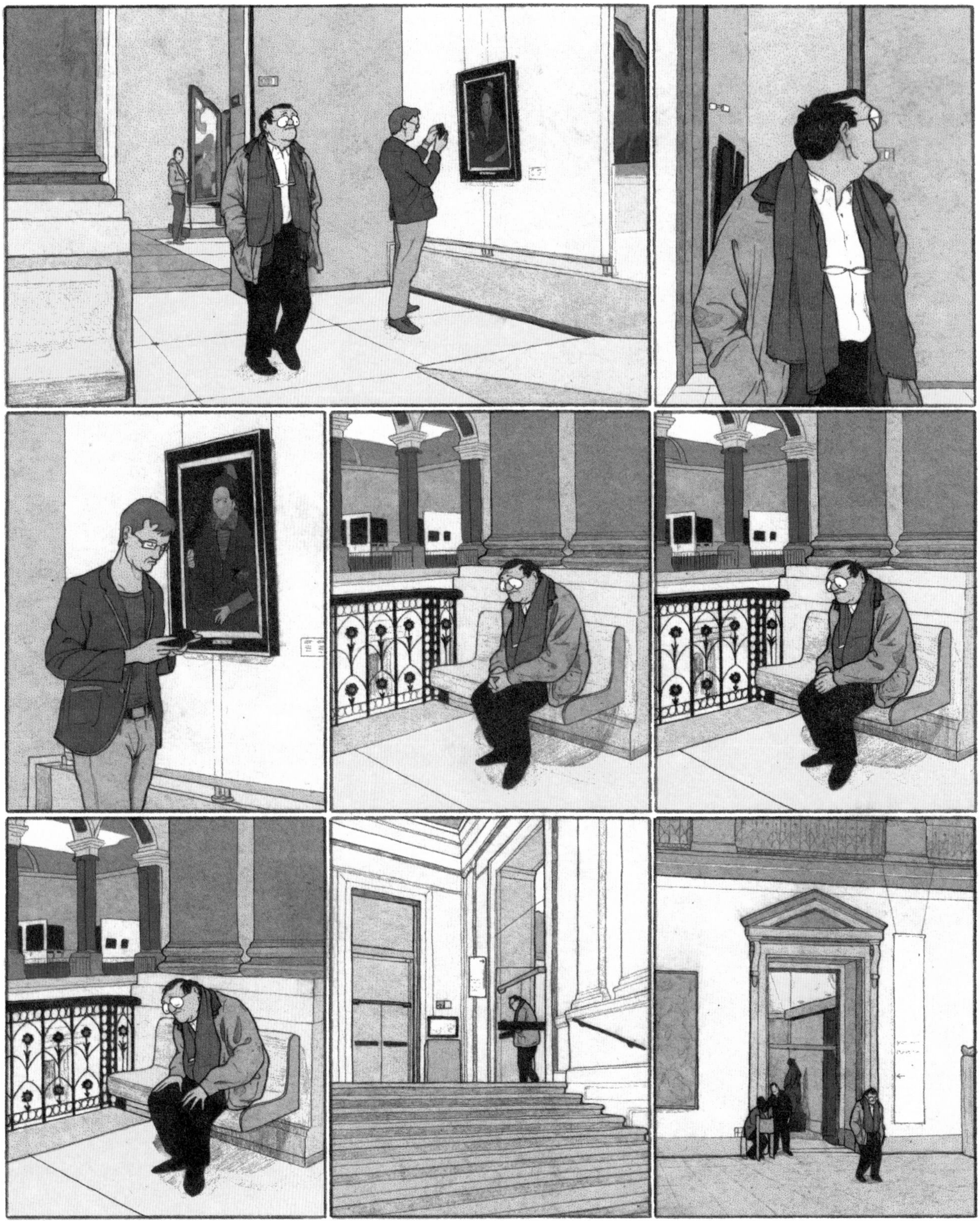

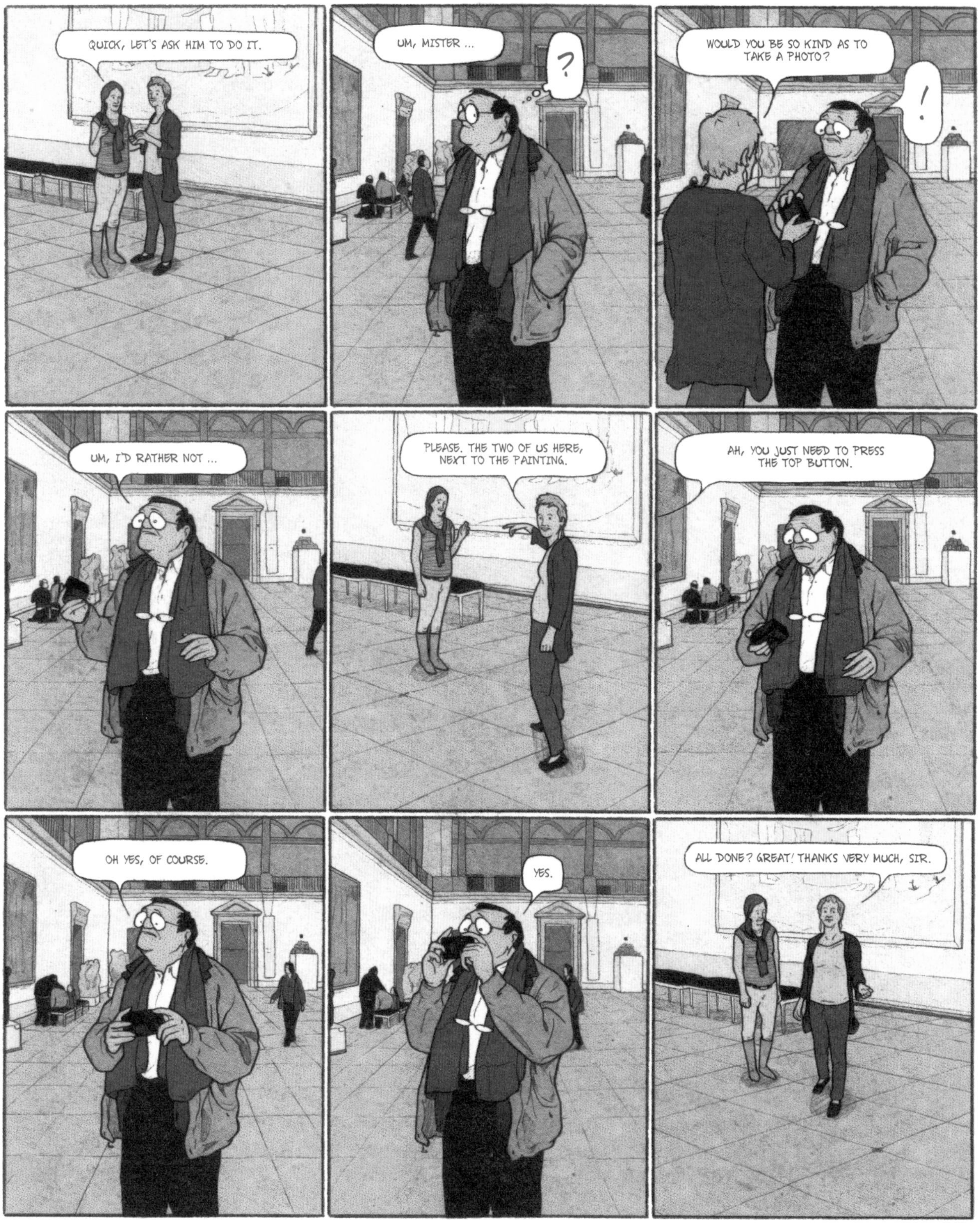
QUICK, LET'S ASK HIM TO DO IT.
UM, MISTER ...
?
WOULD YOU BE SO KIND AS TO TAKE A PHOTO?
!
UM, I'D RATHER NOT ...
PLEASE. THE TWO OF US HERE, NEXT TO THE PAINTING.
AH, YOU JUST NEED TO PRESS THE TOP BUTTON.
OH YES, OF COURSE.
YES.
ALL DONE? GREAT! THANKS VERY MUCH, SIR.

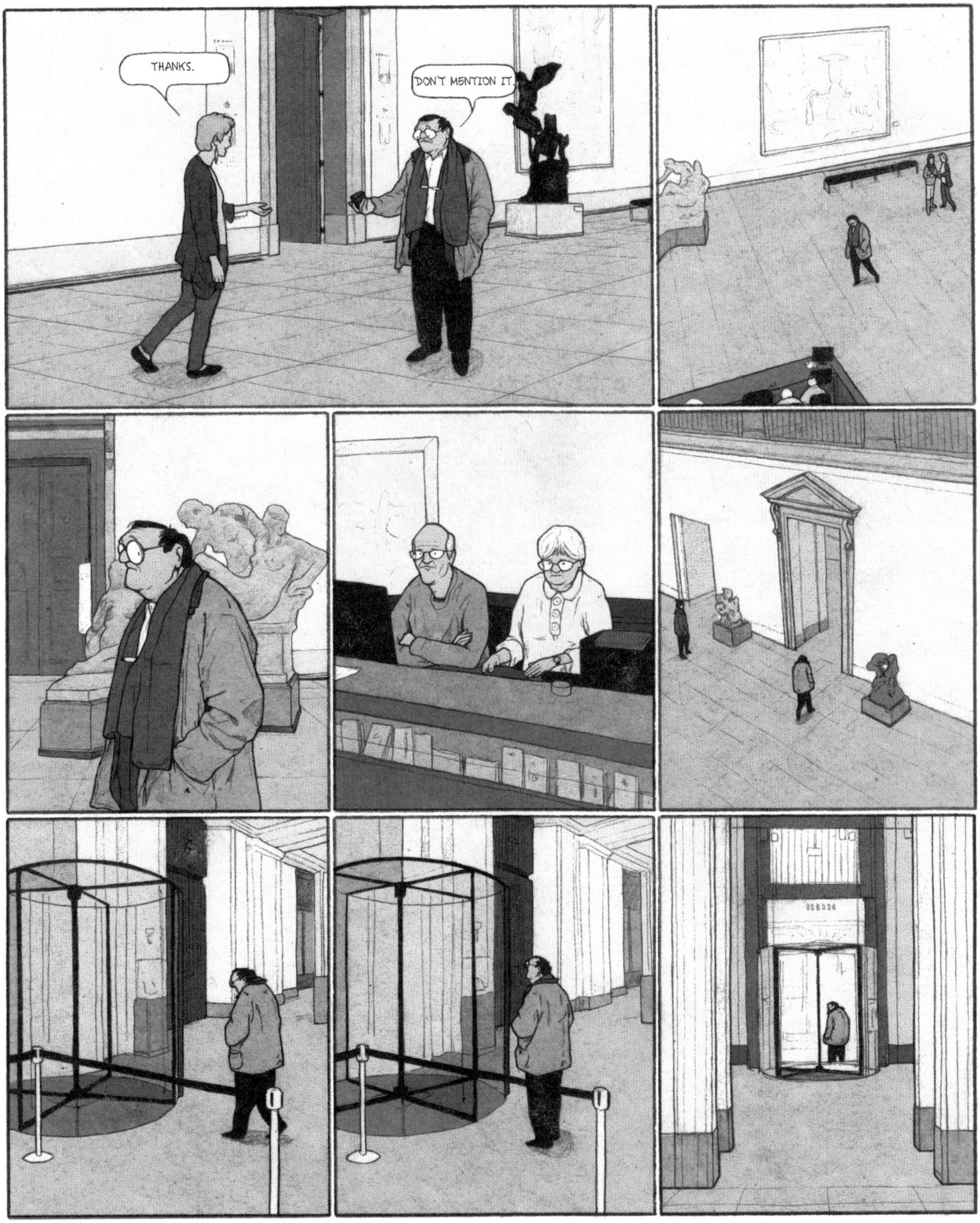
THANKS.
DON'T MENTION IT.

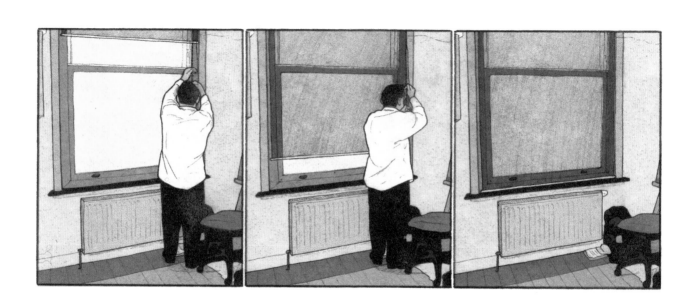

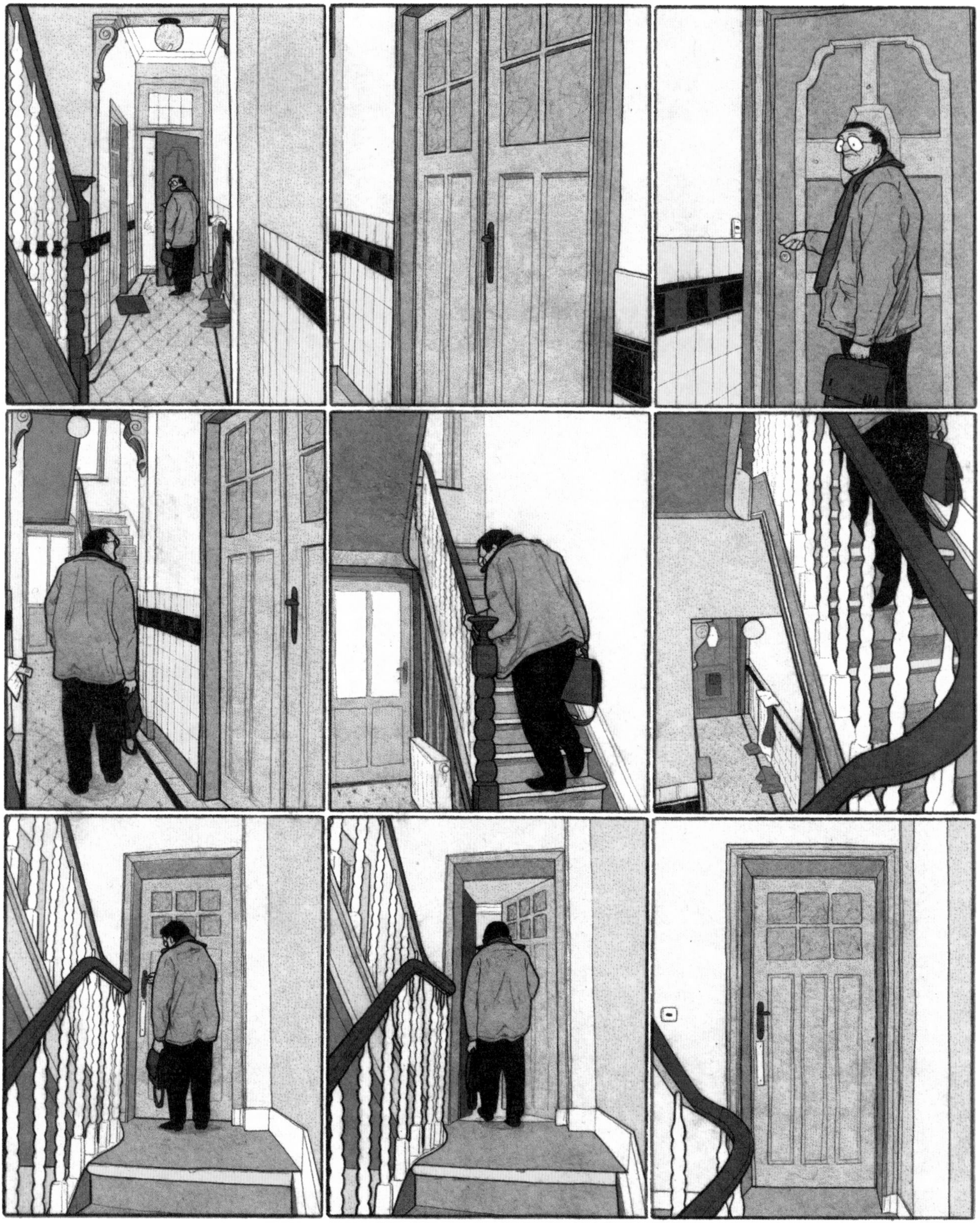

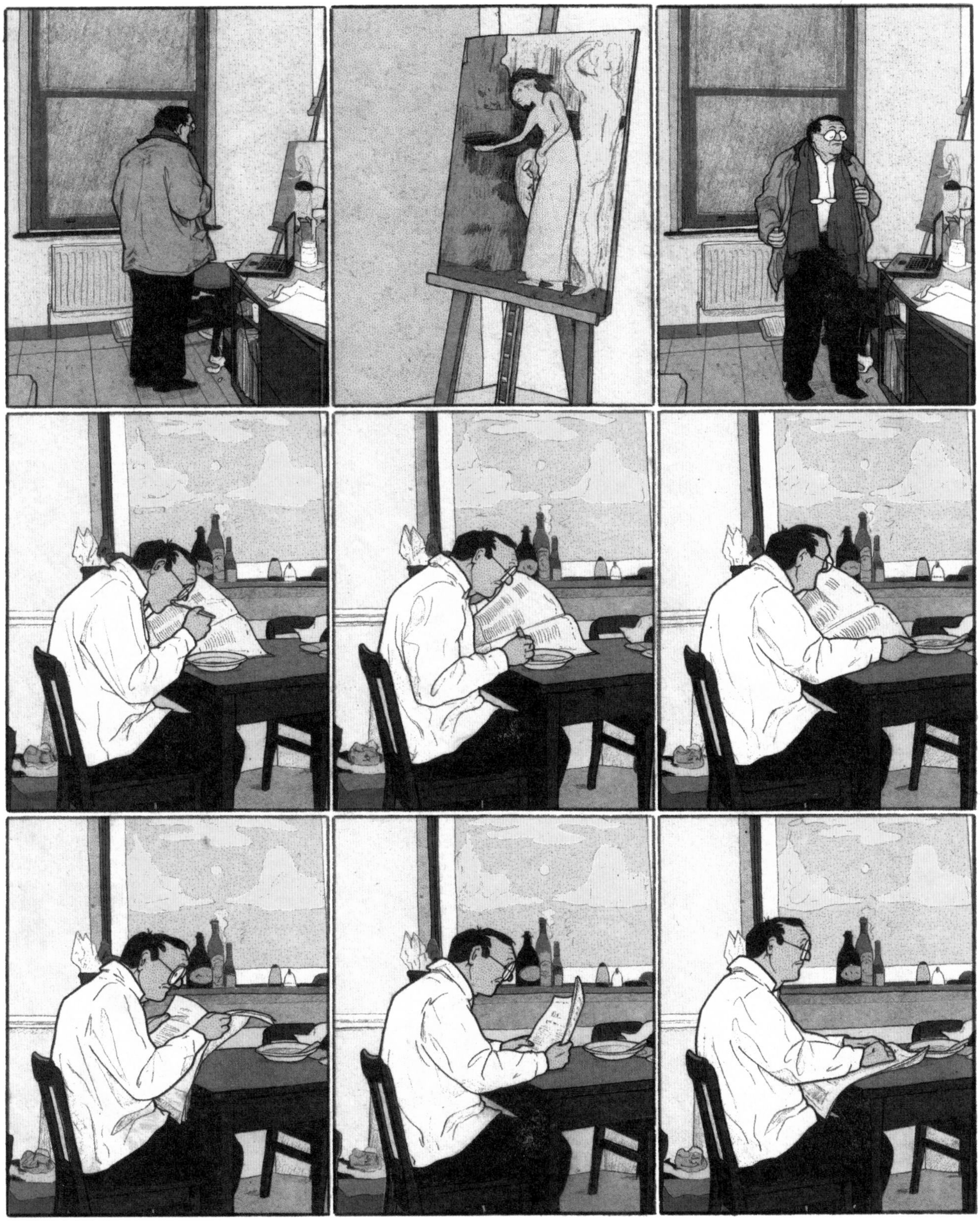

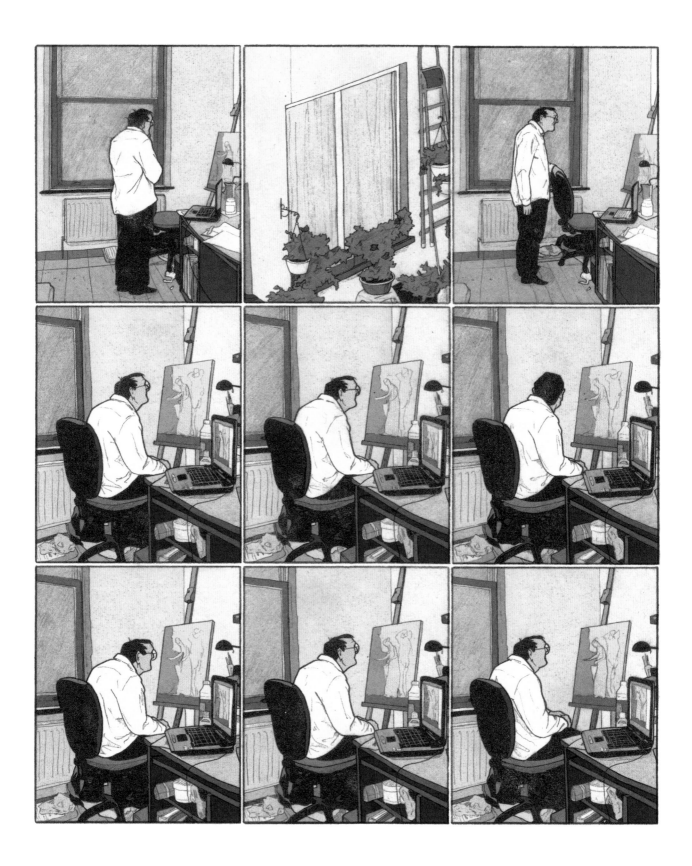

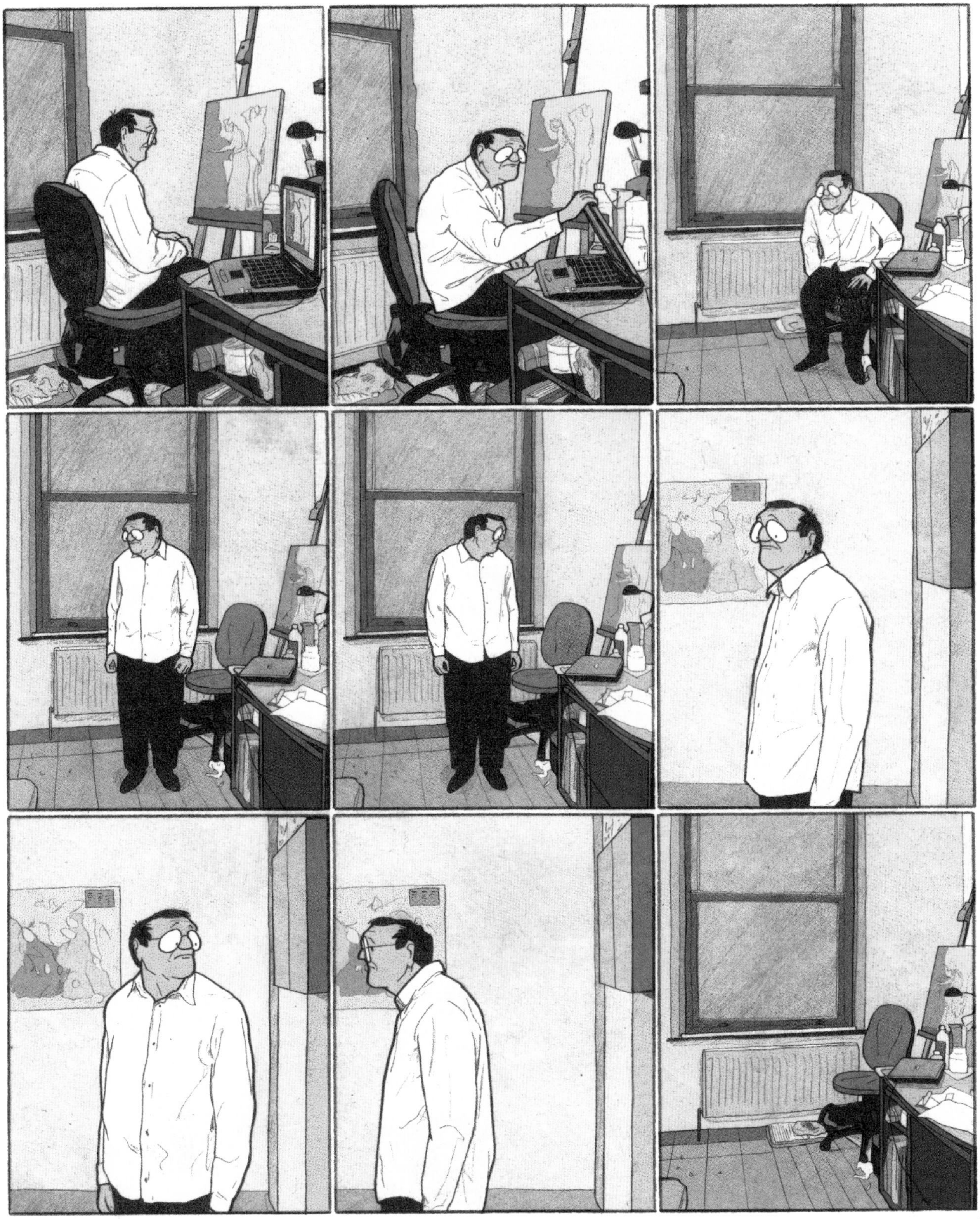

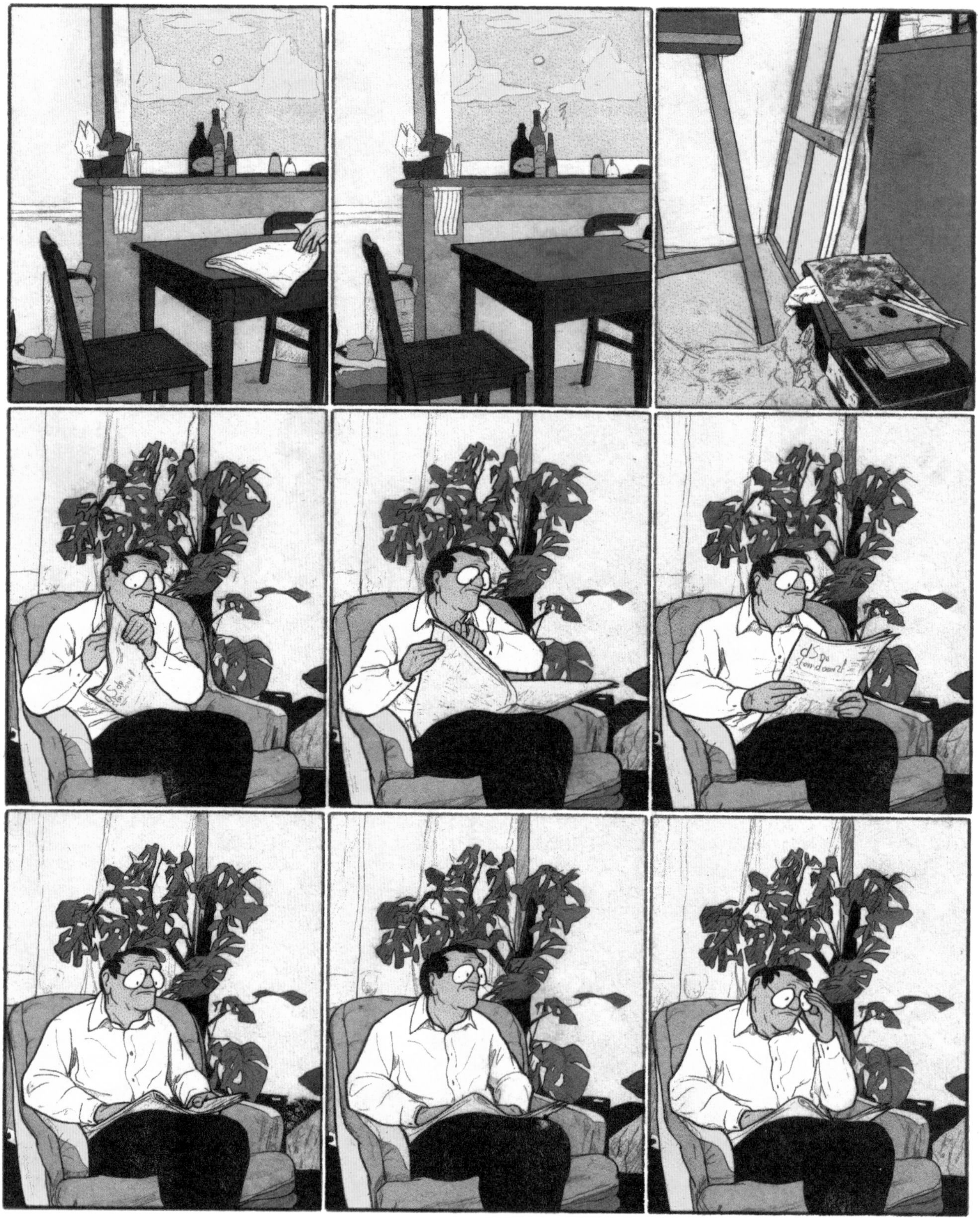
dS De Standaard

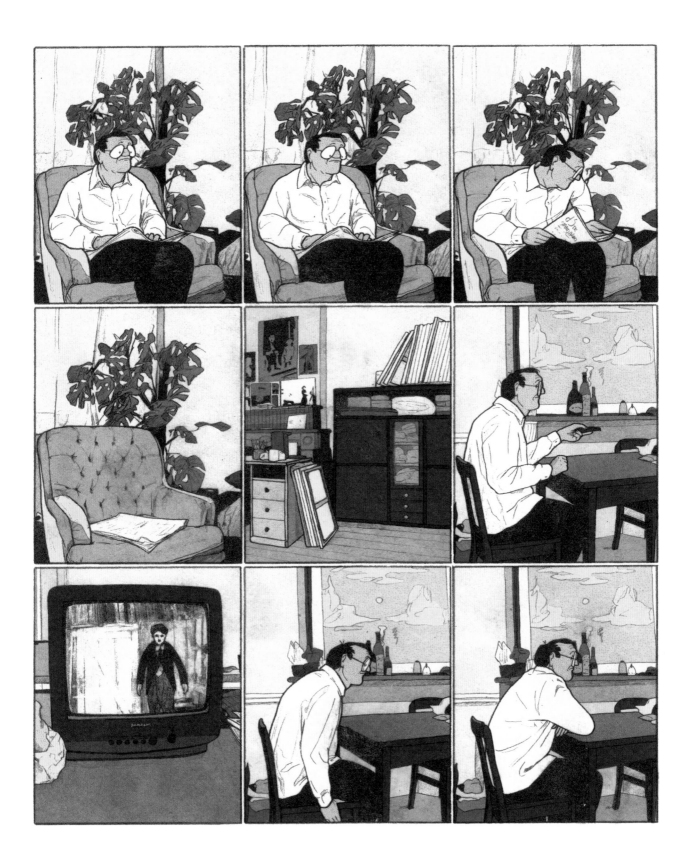

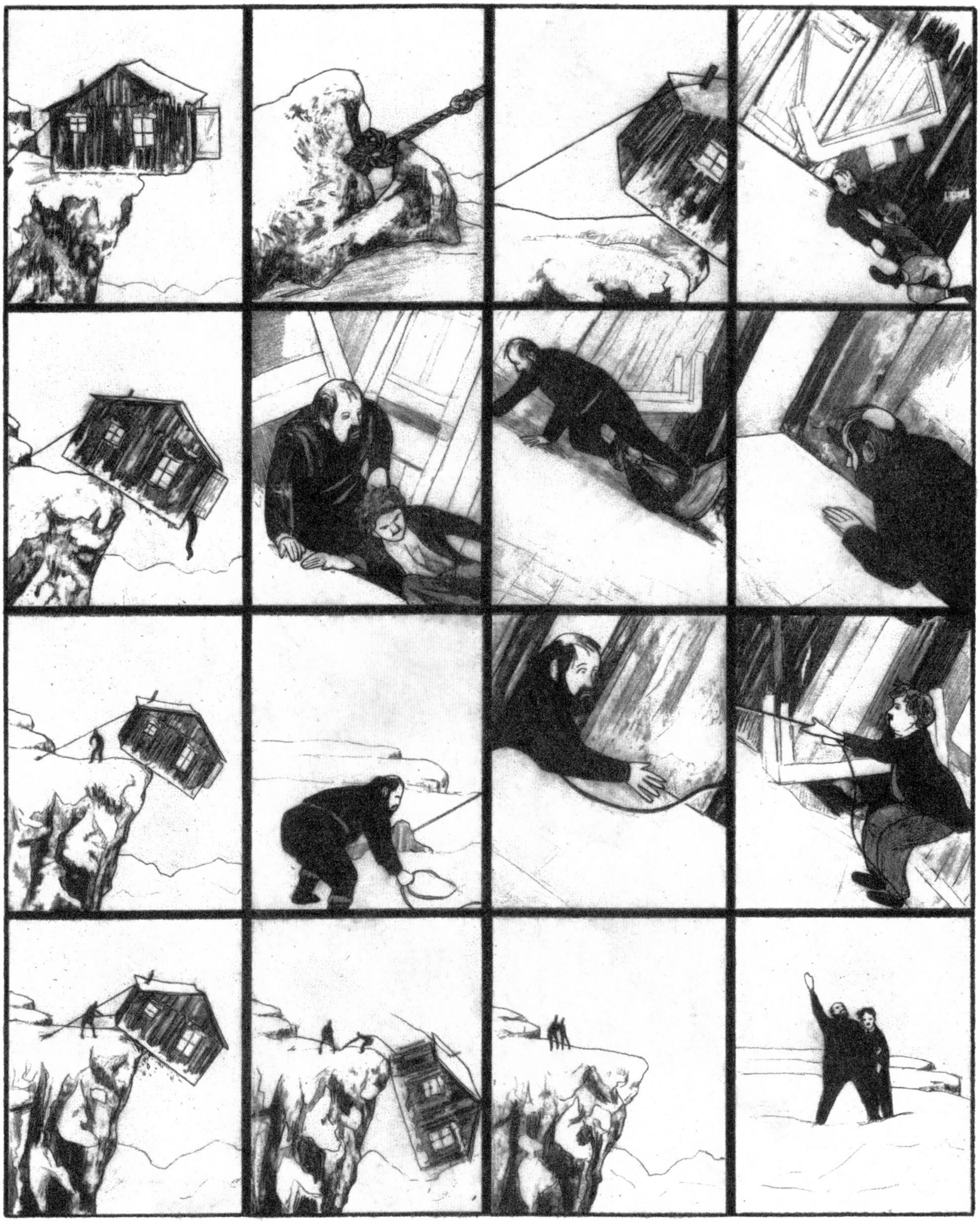

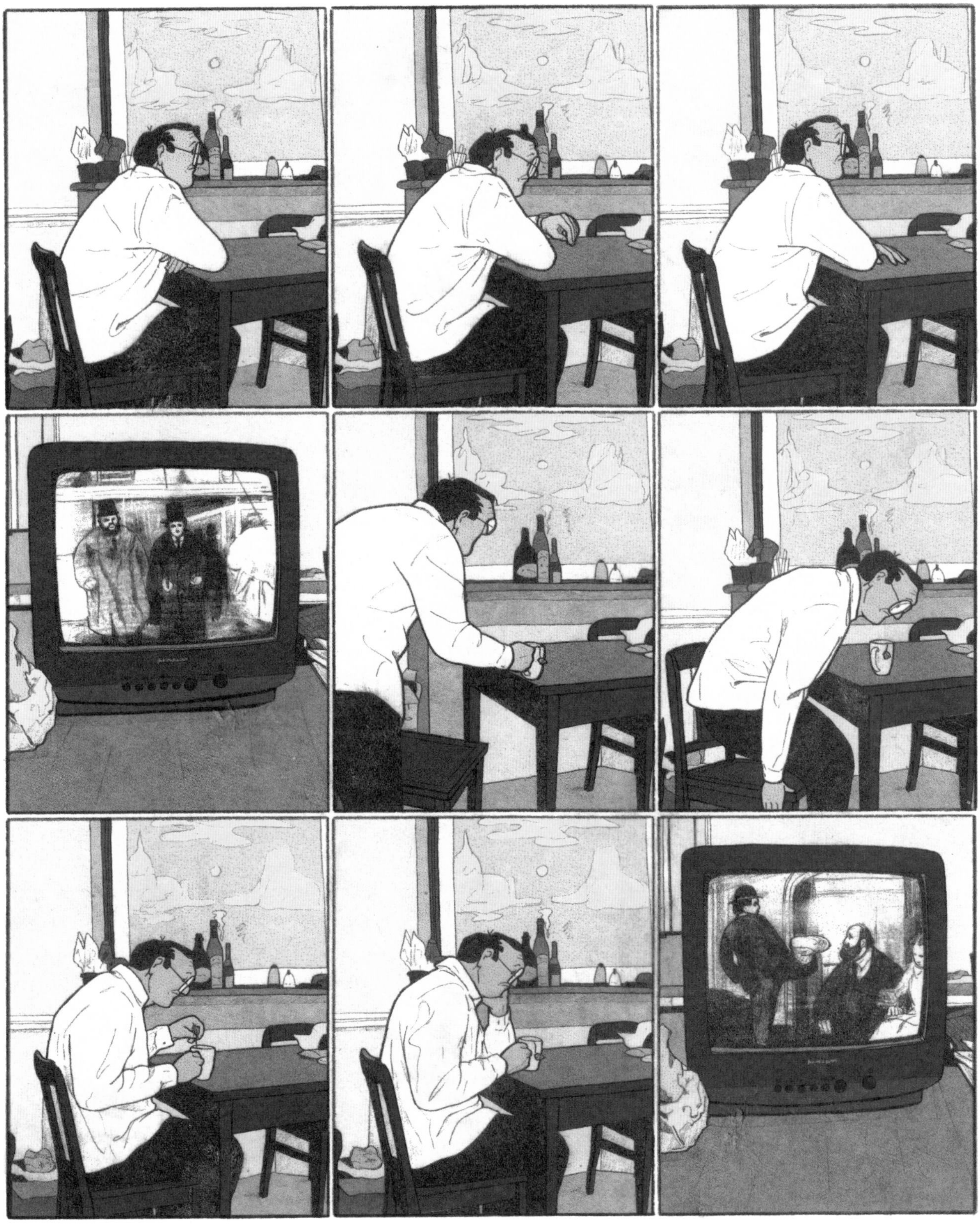

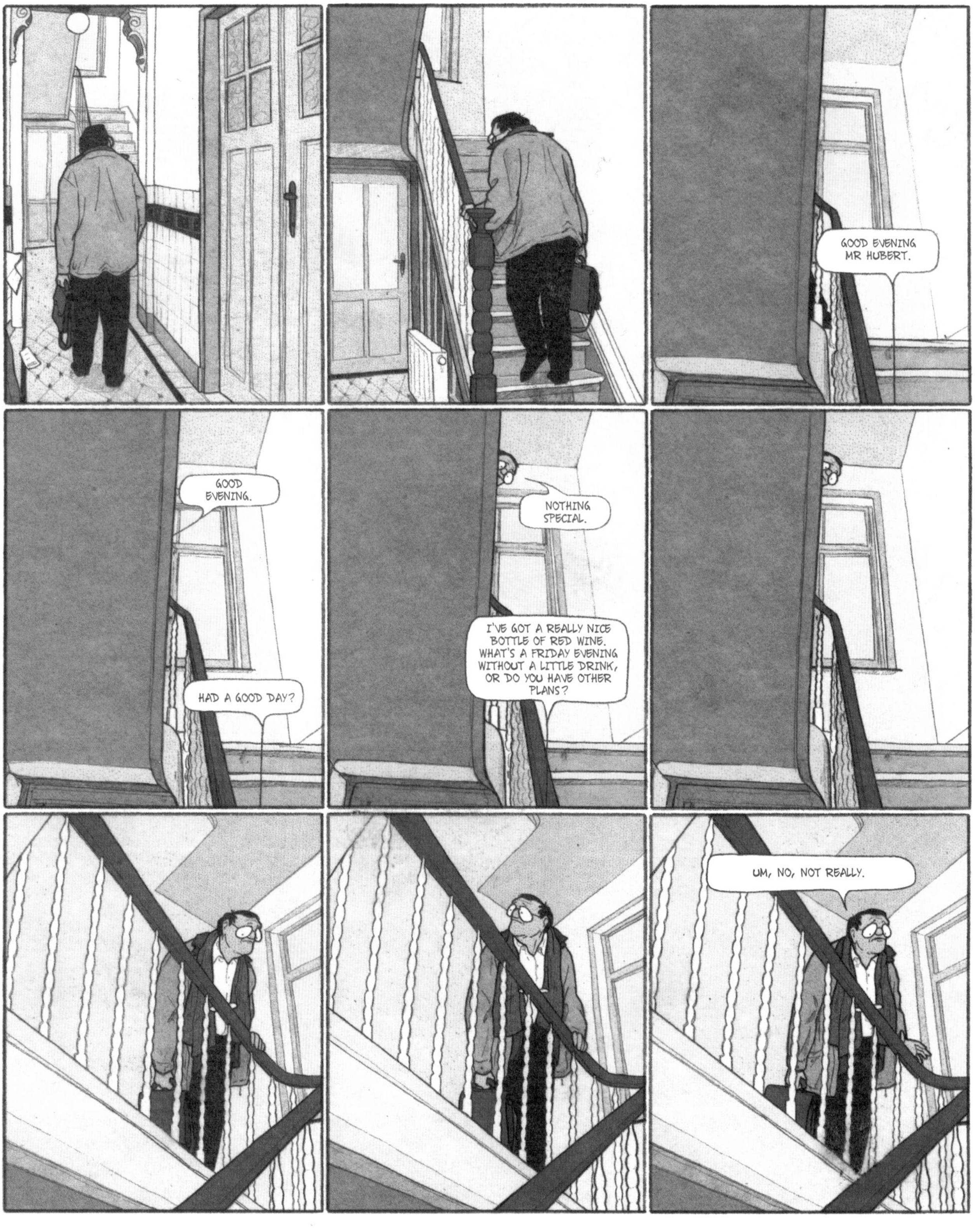
GOOD EVENING MR HUBERT.
GOOD EVENING.
HAD A GOOD DAY?
NOTHING SPECIAL.
I'VE GOT A REALLY NICE BOTTLE OF RED WINE. WHAT'S A FRIDAY EVENING WITHOUT A LITTLE DRINK, OR DO YOU HAVE OTHER PLANS?
UM, NO, NOT REALLY.

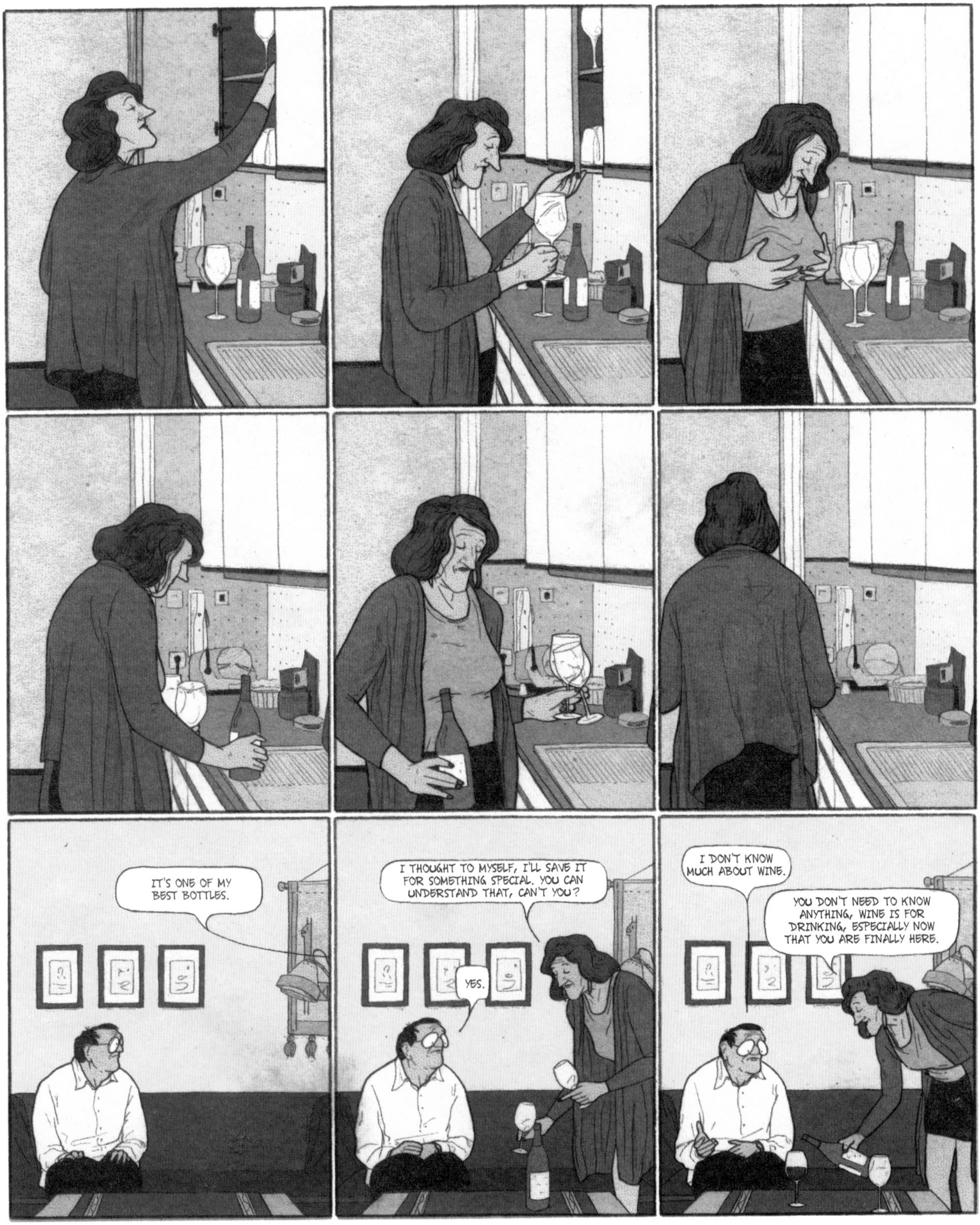
IT'S ONE OF MY BEST BOTTLES.
I THOUGHT TO MYSELF, I'LL SAVE IT FOR SOMETHING SPECIAL. YOU CAN UNDERSTAND THAT, CAN'T YOU?
YES.
I DON'T KNOW MUCH ABOUT WINE.
YOU DON'T NEED TO KNOW ANYTHING, WINE IS FOR DRINKING, ESPECIALLY NOW THAT YOU ARE FINALLY HERE.

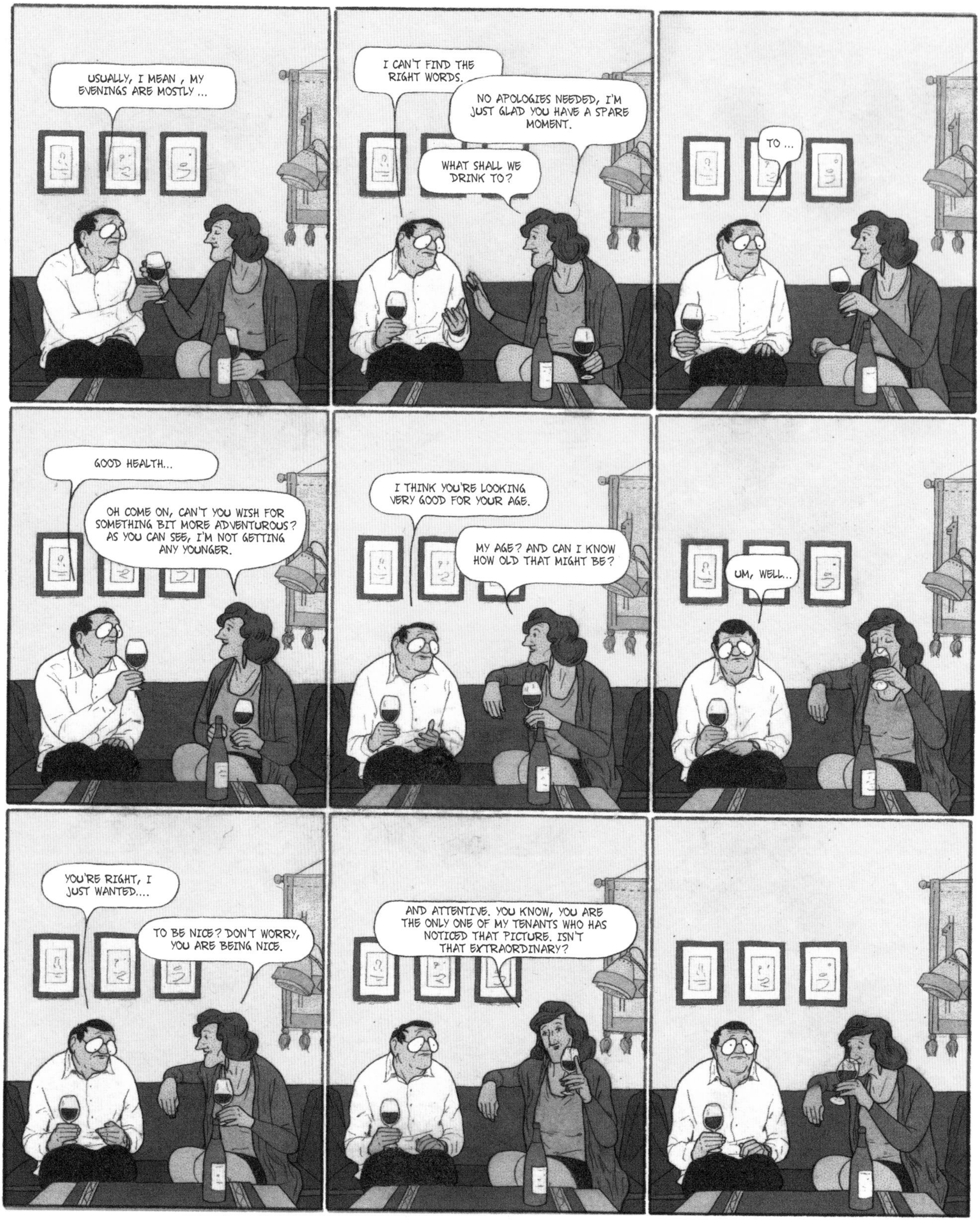
USUALLY, I MEAN , MY EVENINGS ARE MOSTLY ...
I CAN'T FIND THE RIGHT WORDS.
NO APOLOGIES NEEDED, I'M JUST GLAD YOU HAVE A SPARE MOMENT.
WHAT SHALL WE DRINK TO?
TO ...
GOOD HEALTH...
OH COME ON, CAN'T YOU WISH FOR SOMETHING BIT MORE ADVENTUROUS? AS YOU CAN SEE, I'M NOT GETTING ANY YOUNGER.
I THINK YOU'RE LOOKING VERY GOOD FOR YOUR AGE.
MY AGE? AND CAN I KNOW HOW OLD THAT MIGHT BE?
UM, WELL...
YOU'RE RIGHT, I JUST WANTED....
TO BE NICE? DON'T WORRY, YOU ARE BEING NICE.
AND ATTENTIVE. YOU KNOW, YOU ARE THE ONLY ONE OF MY TENANTS WHO HAS NOTICED THAT PICTURE. ISN'T THAT EXTRAORDINARY?

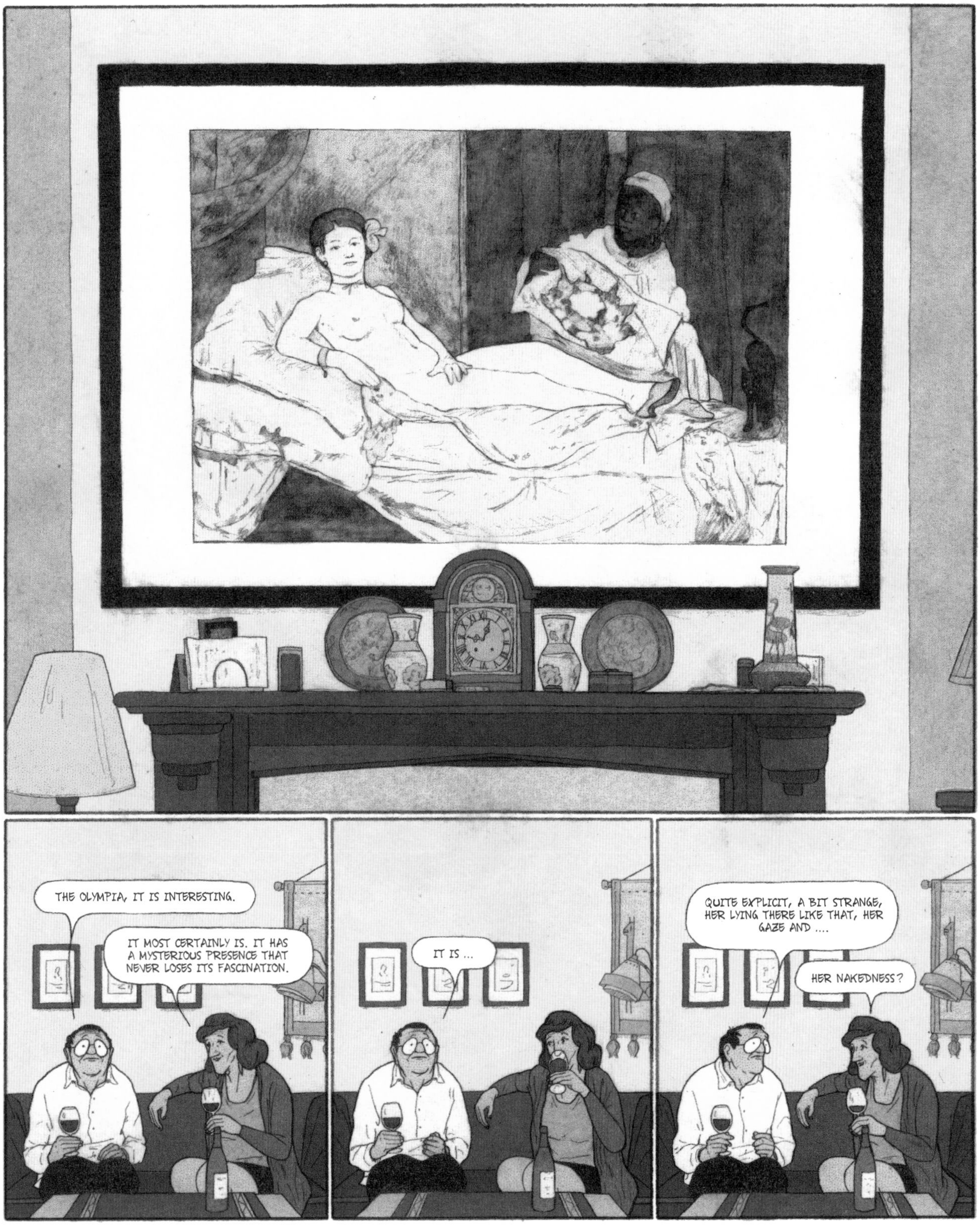
THE OLYMPIA, IT IS INTERESTING.
IT MOST CERTAINLY IS. IT HAS A MYSTERIOUS PRESENCE THAT NEVER LOSES ITS FASCINATION.
IT IS ...
QUITE EXPLICIT, A BIT STRANGE, HER LYING THERE LIKE THAT, HER GAZE AND ....
HER NAKEDNESS?

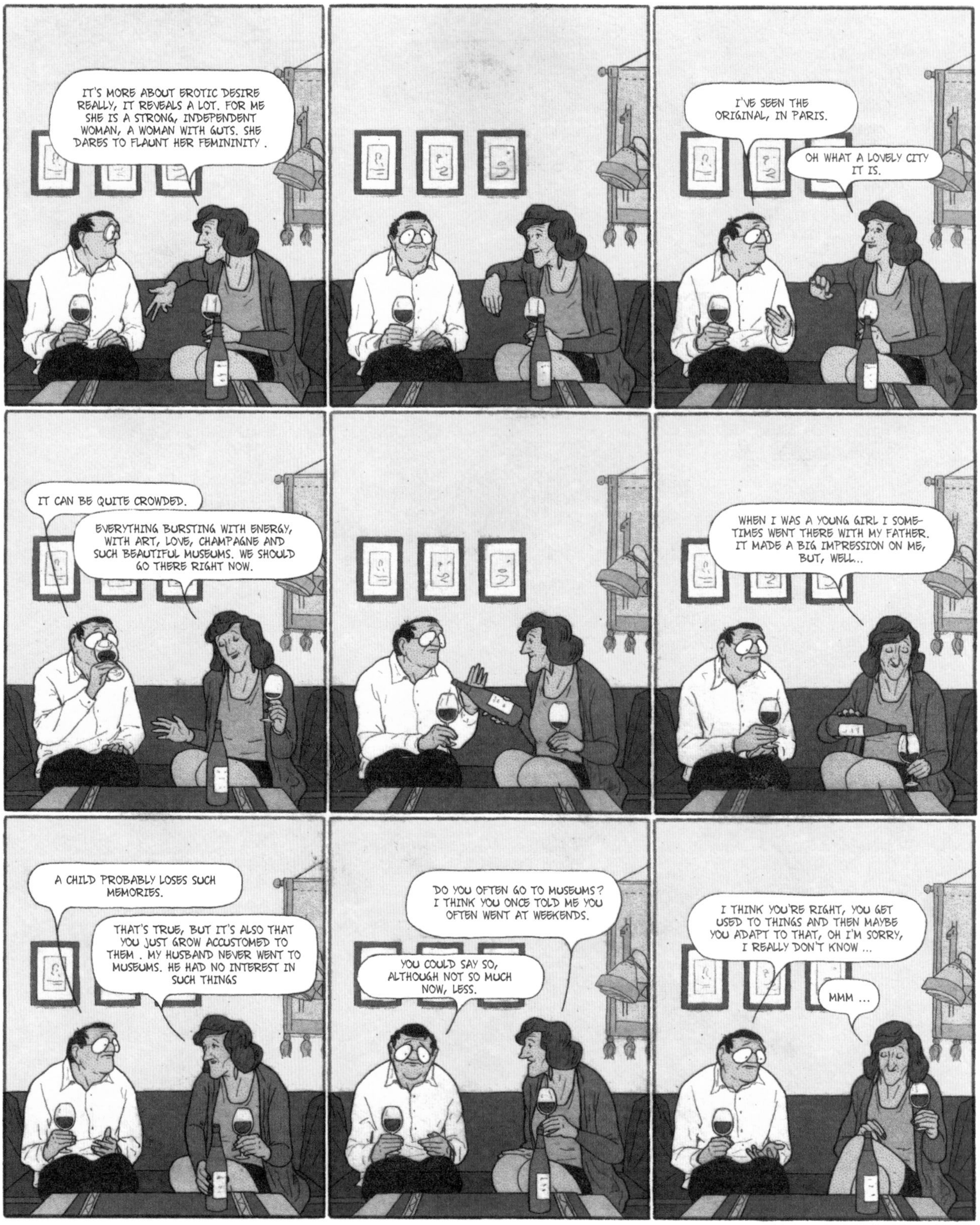
IT'S MORE ABOUT EROTIC DESIRE REALLY, IT REVEALS A LOT. FOR ME SHE IS A STRONG, INDEPENDENT WOMAN, A WOMAN WITH GUTS. SHE DARES TO FLAUNT HER FEMININITY .
I'VE SEEN THE ORIGINAL, IN PARIS.
OH WHAT A LOVELY CITY IT IS.
IT CAN BE QUITE CROWDED.
EVERYTHING BURSTING WITH ENERGY, WITH ART, LOVE, CHAMPAGNE AND SUCH BEAUTIFUL MUSEUMS. WE SHOULD GO THERE RIGHT NOW.
WHEN I WAS A YOUNG GIRL I SOME-TIMES WENT THERE WITH MY FATHER. IT MADE A BIG IMPRESSION ON ME, BUT, WELL...
A CHILD PROBABLY LOSES SUCH MEMORIES.
THAT'S TRUE, BUT IT'S ALSO THAT YOU JUST GROW ACCUSTOMED TO THEM . MY HUSBAND NEVER WENT TO MUSEUMS. HE HAD NO INTEREST IN SUCH THINGS
DO YOU OFTEN GO TO MUSEUMS? I THINK YOU ONCE TOLD ME YOU OFTEN WENT AT WEEKENDS.
YOU COULD SAY SO, ALTHOUGH NOT SO MUCH NOW, LESS.
I THINK YOU'RE RIGHT, YOU GET USED TO THINGS AND THEN MAYBE YOU ADAPT TO THAT, OH I'M SORRY, I REALLY DON'T KNOW ...
MMM ...

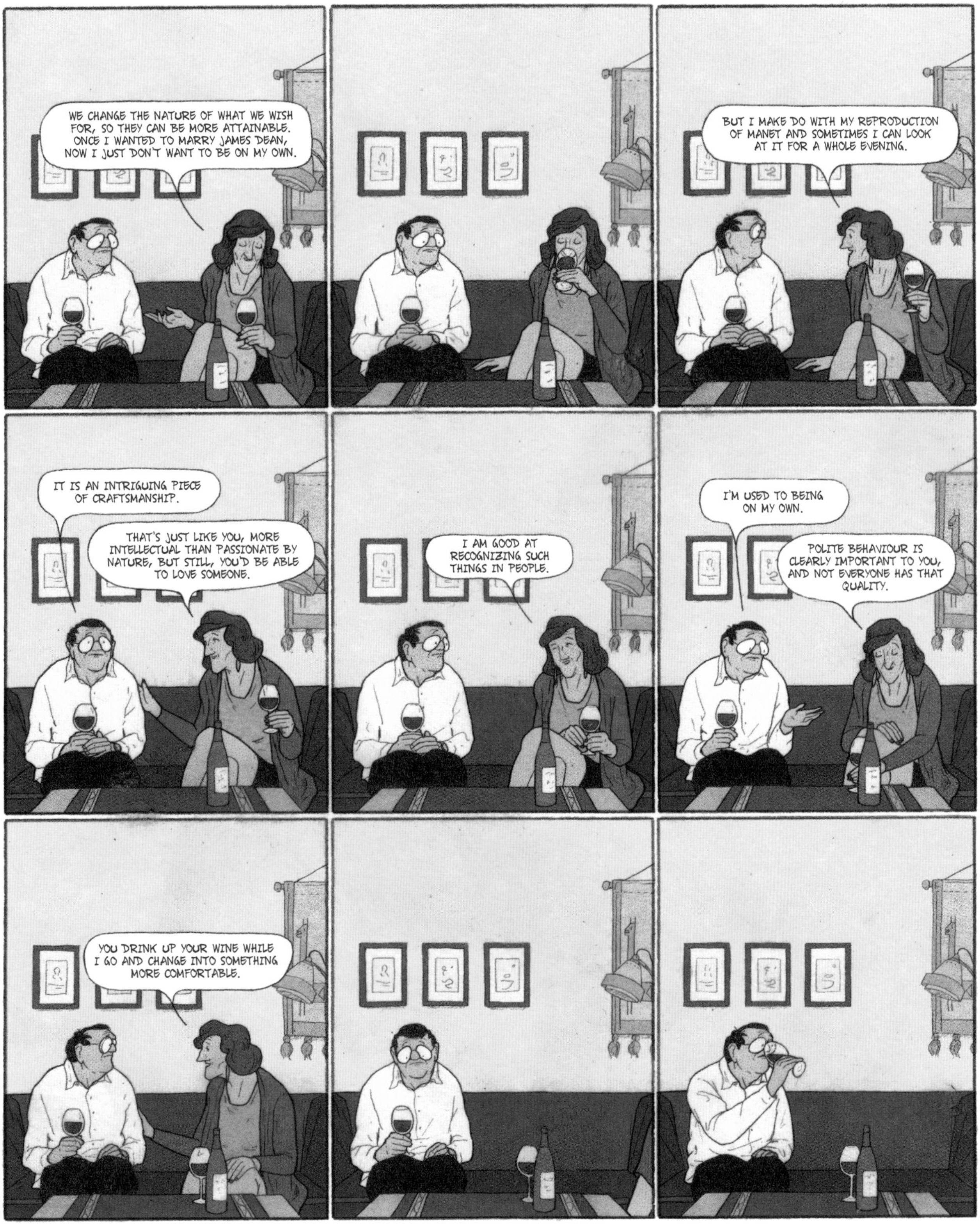
WE CHANGE THE NATURE OF WHAT WE WISH FOR, SO THEY CAN BE MORE ATTAINABLE. ONCE I WANTED TO MARRY JAMES DEAN, NOW I JUST DON'T WANT TO BE ON MY OWN.
BUT I MAKE DO WITH MY REPRODUCTION OF MANET AND SOMETIMES I CAN LOOK AT IT FOR A WHOLE EVENING.
IT IS AN INTRIGUING PIECE OF CRAFTSMANSHIP.
THAT'S JUST LIKE YOU, MORE INTELLECTUAL THAN PASSIONATE BY NATURE, BUT STILL, YOU'D BE ABLE TO LOVE SOMEONE.
I AM GOOD AT RECOGNIZING SUCH THINGS IN PEOPLE.
I'M USED TO BEING ON MY OWN.
POLITE BEHAVIOUR IS CLEARLY IMPORTANT TO YOU, AND NOT EVERYONE HAS THAT QUALITY.
YOU DRINK UP YOUR WINE WHILE I GO AND CHANGE INTO SOMETHING MORE COMFORTABLE.

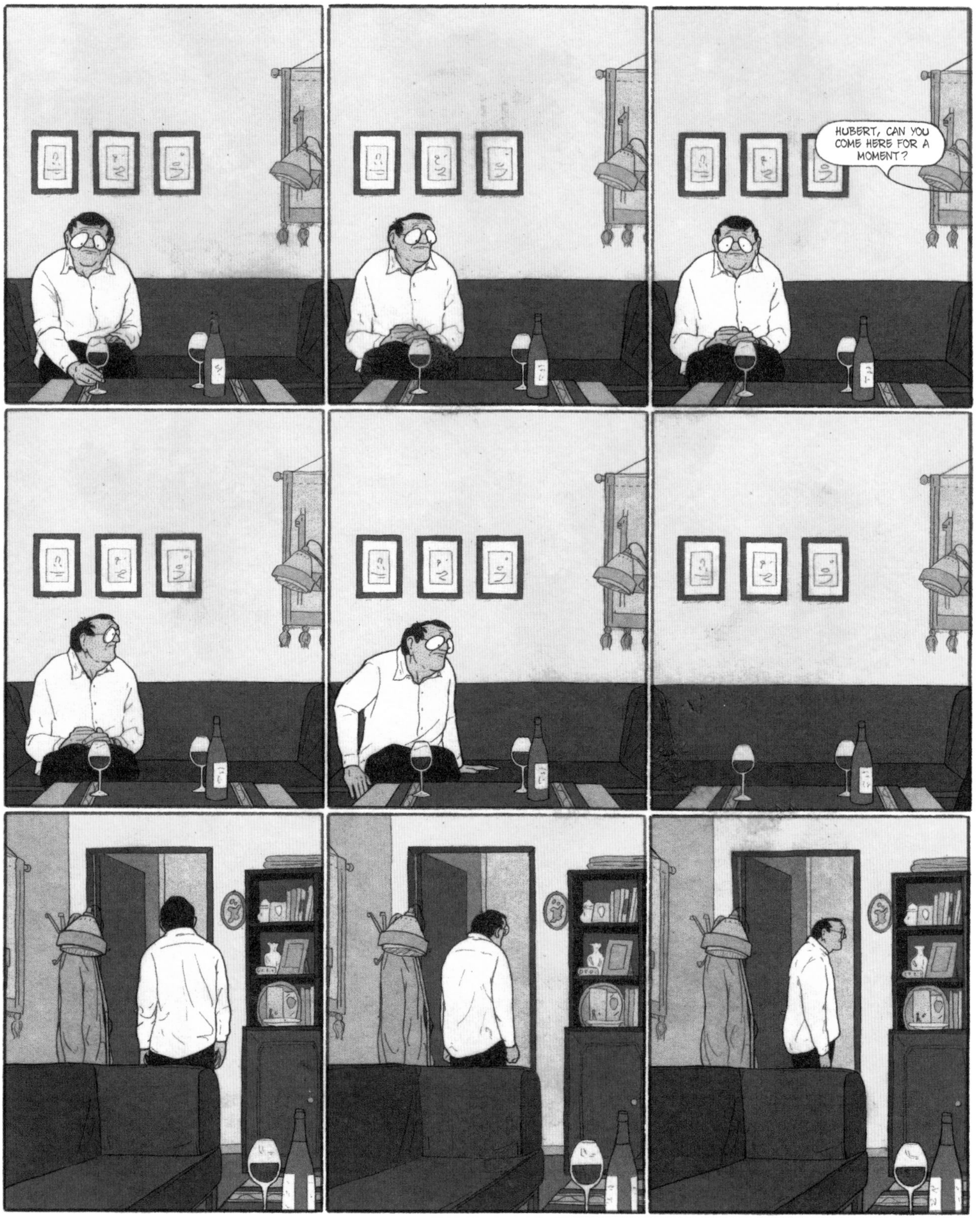
HUBERT, CAN YOU COME HERE FOR A MOMENT?

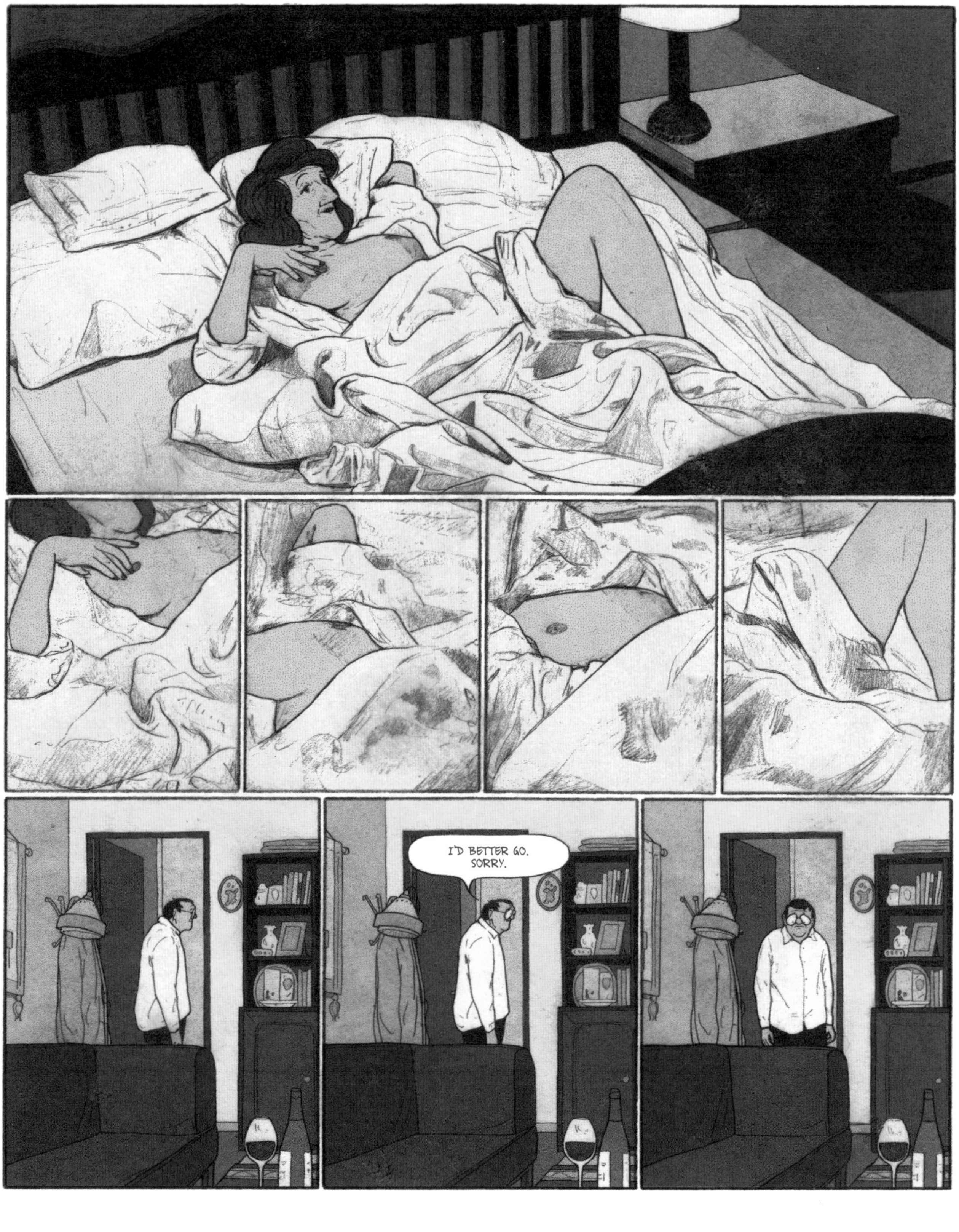
I'D BETTER GO.
SORRY.

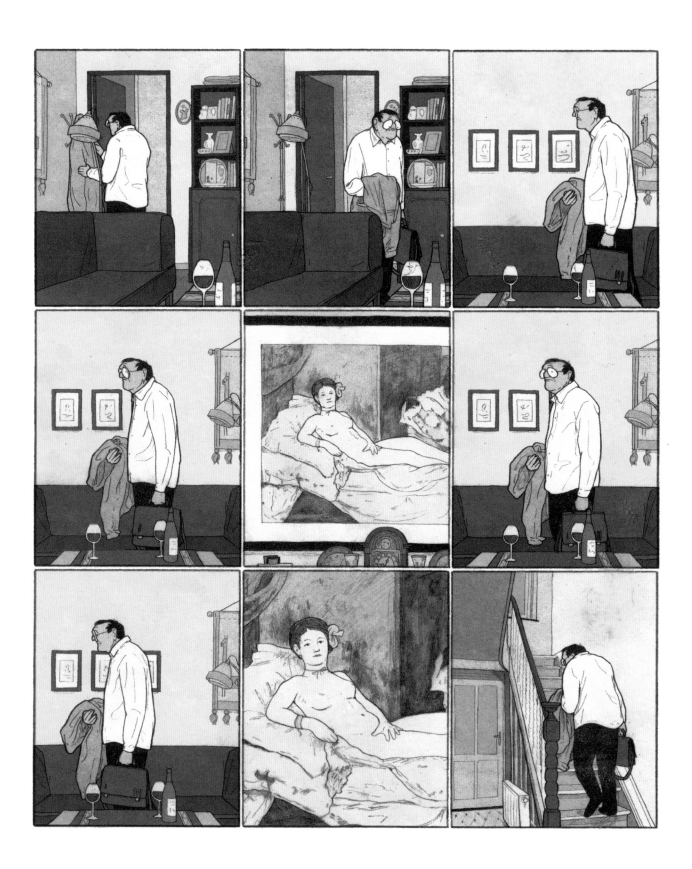

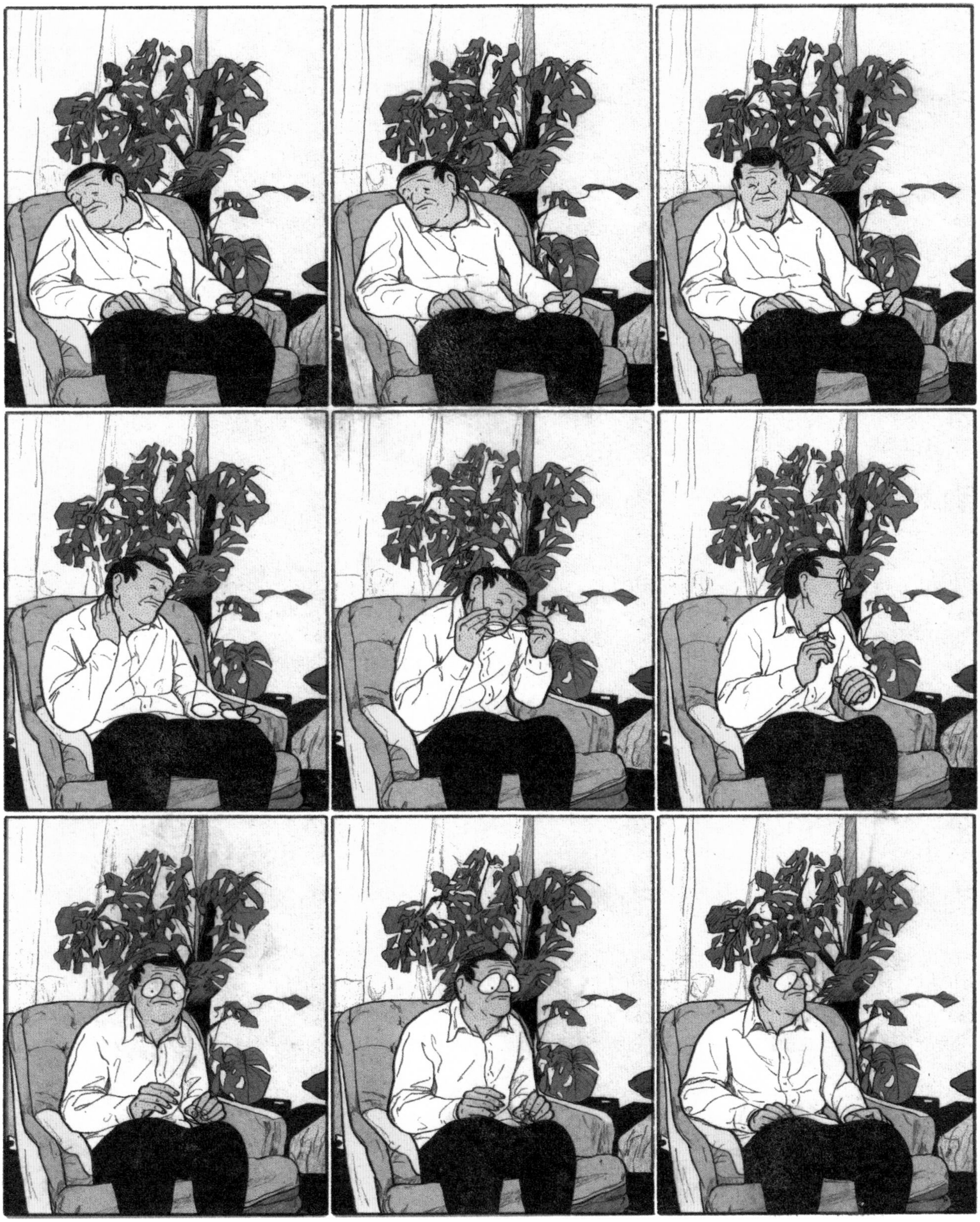

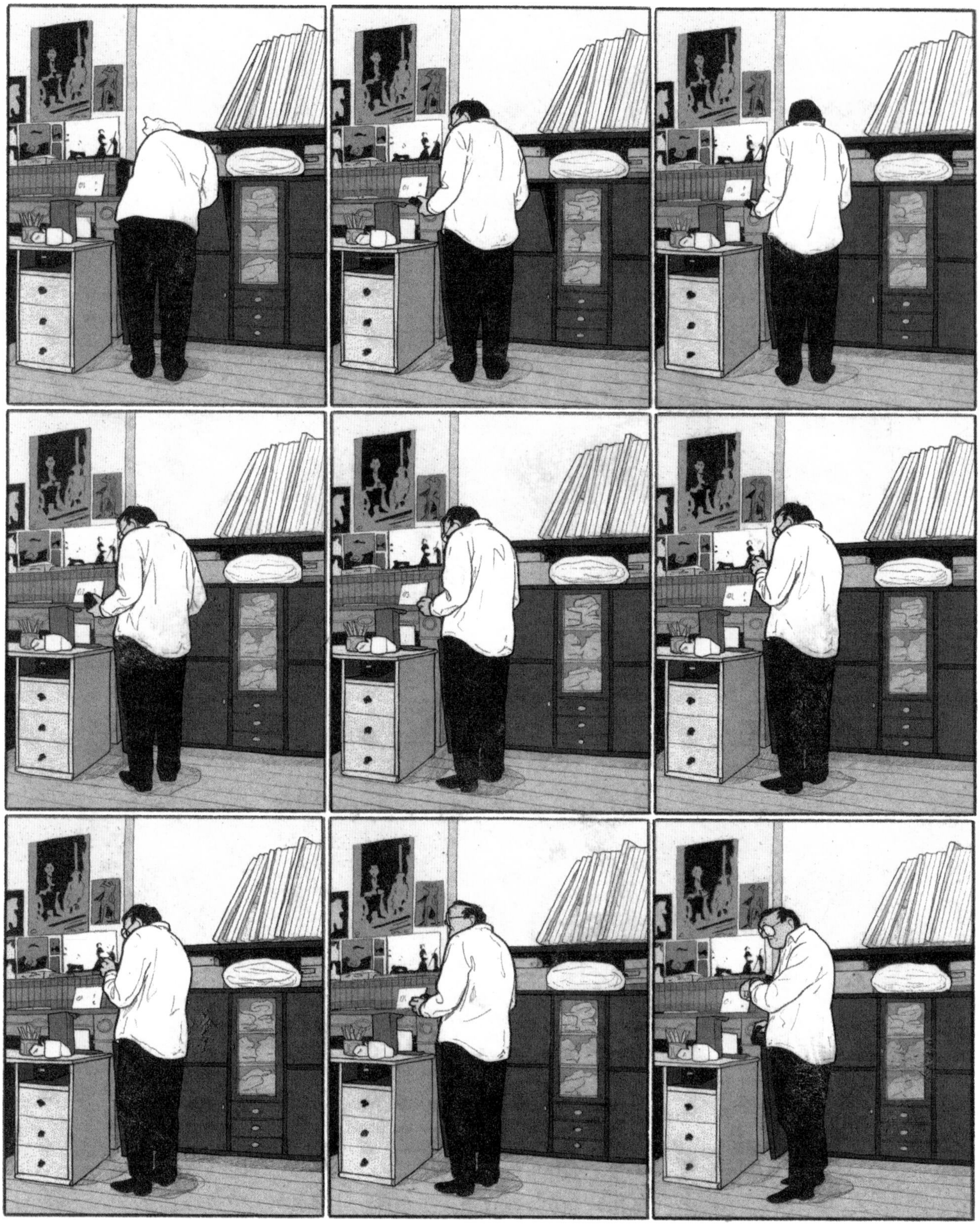

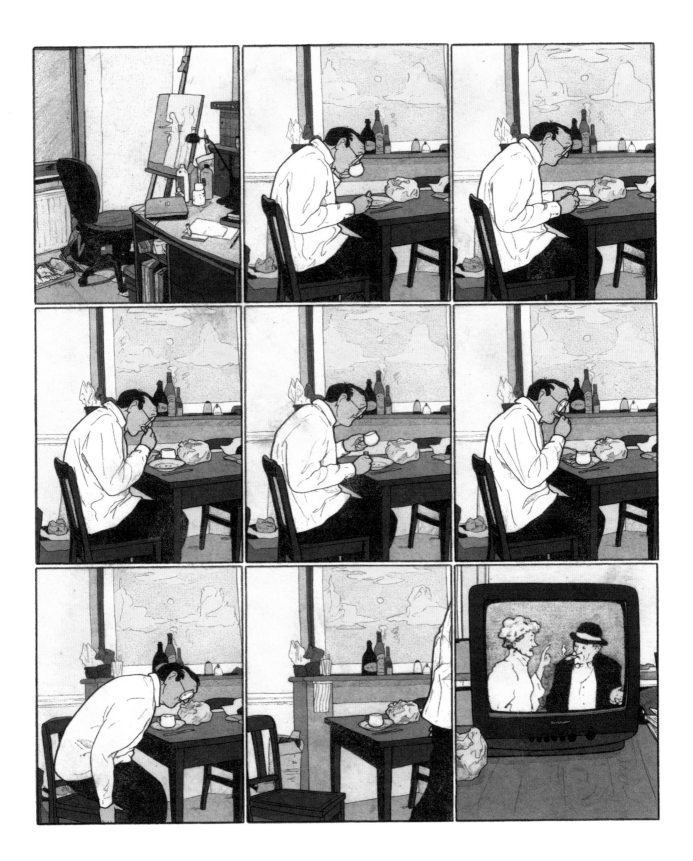

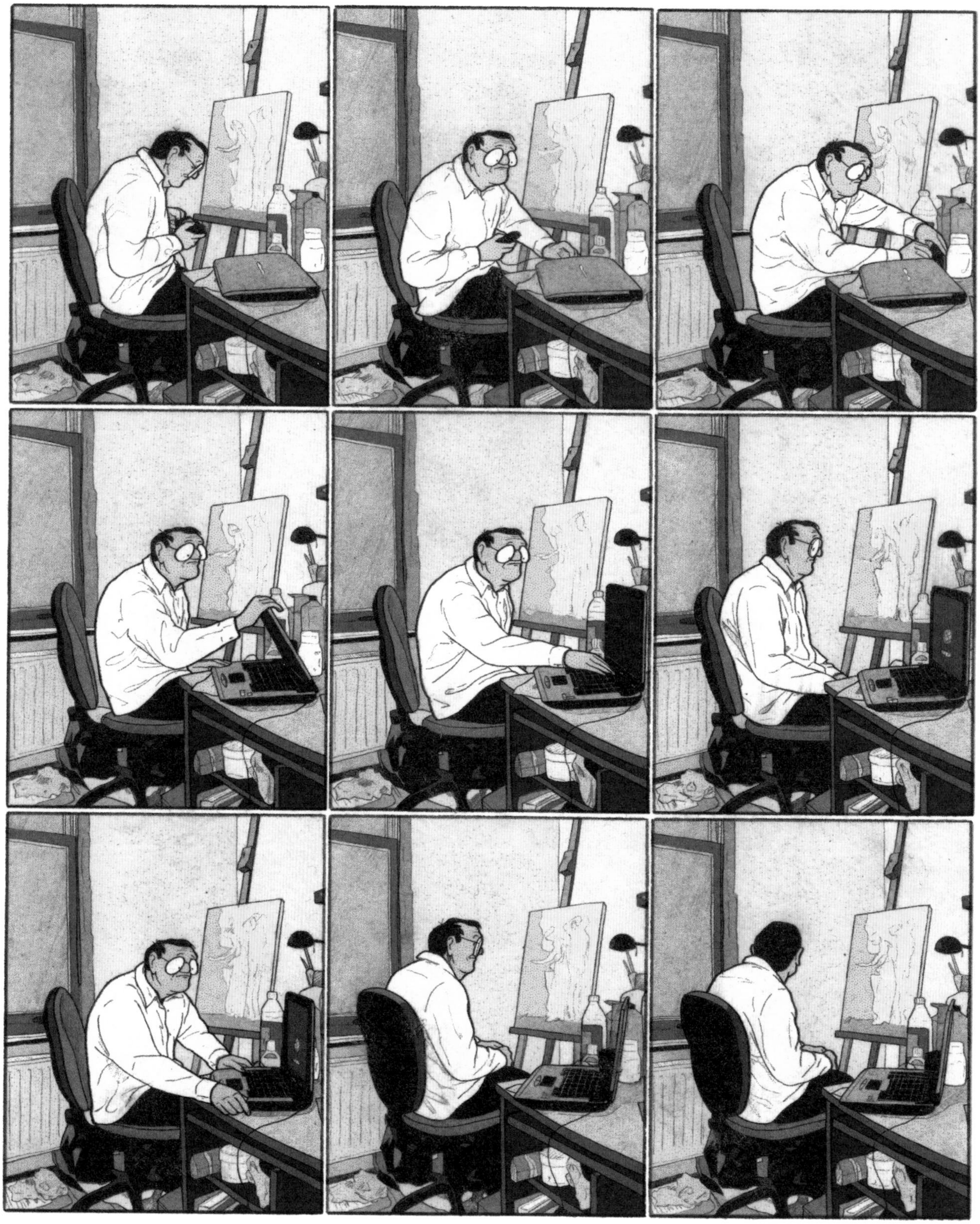

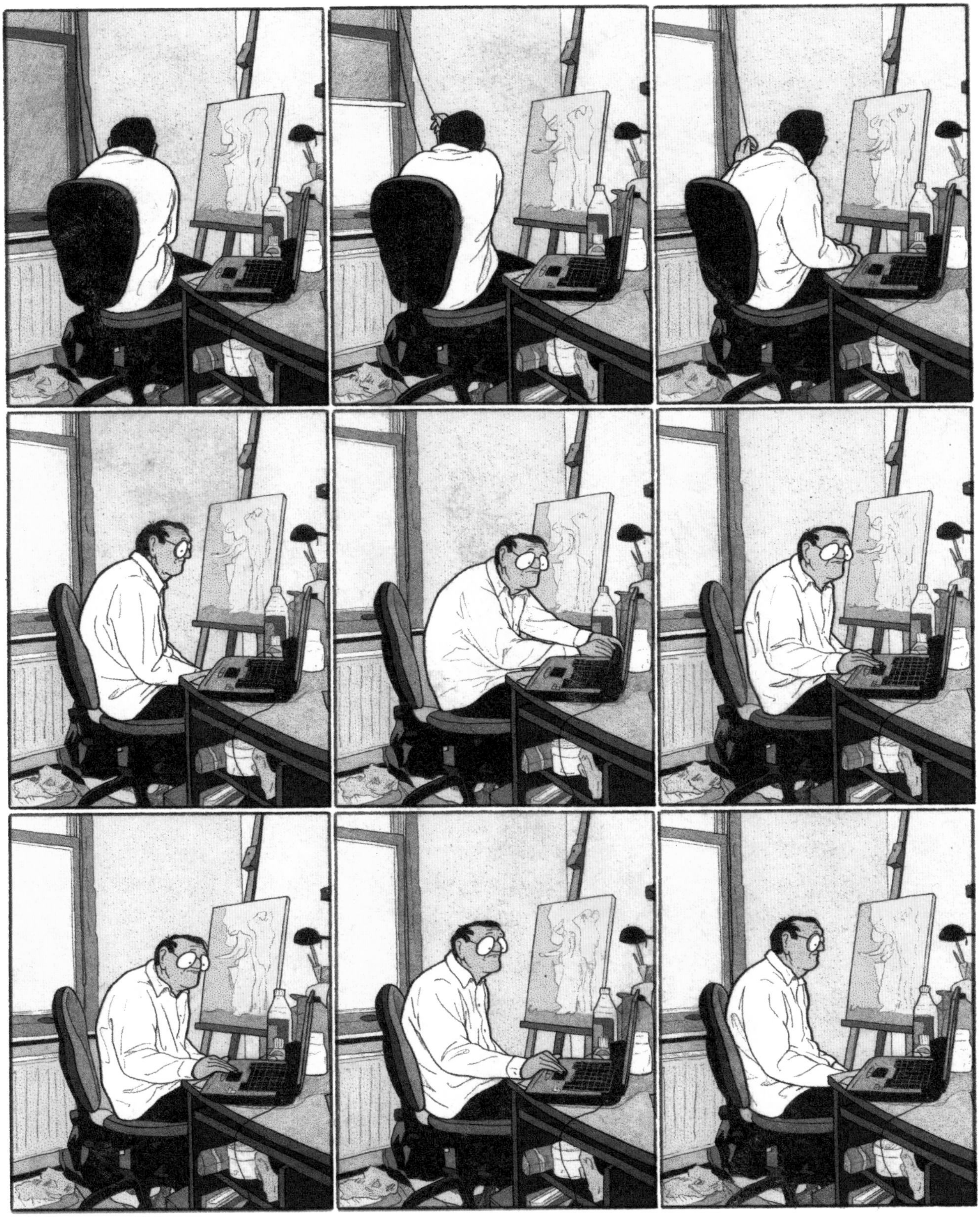

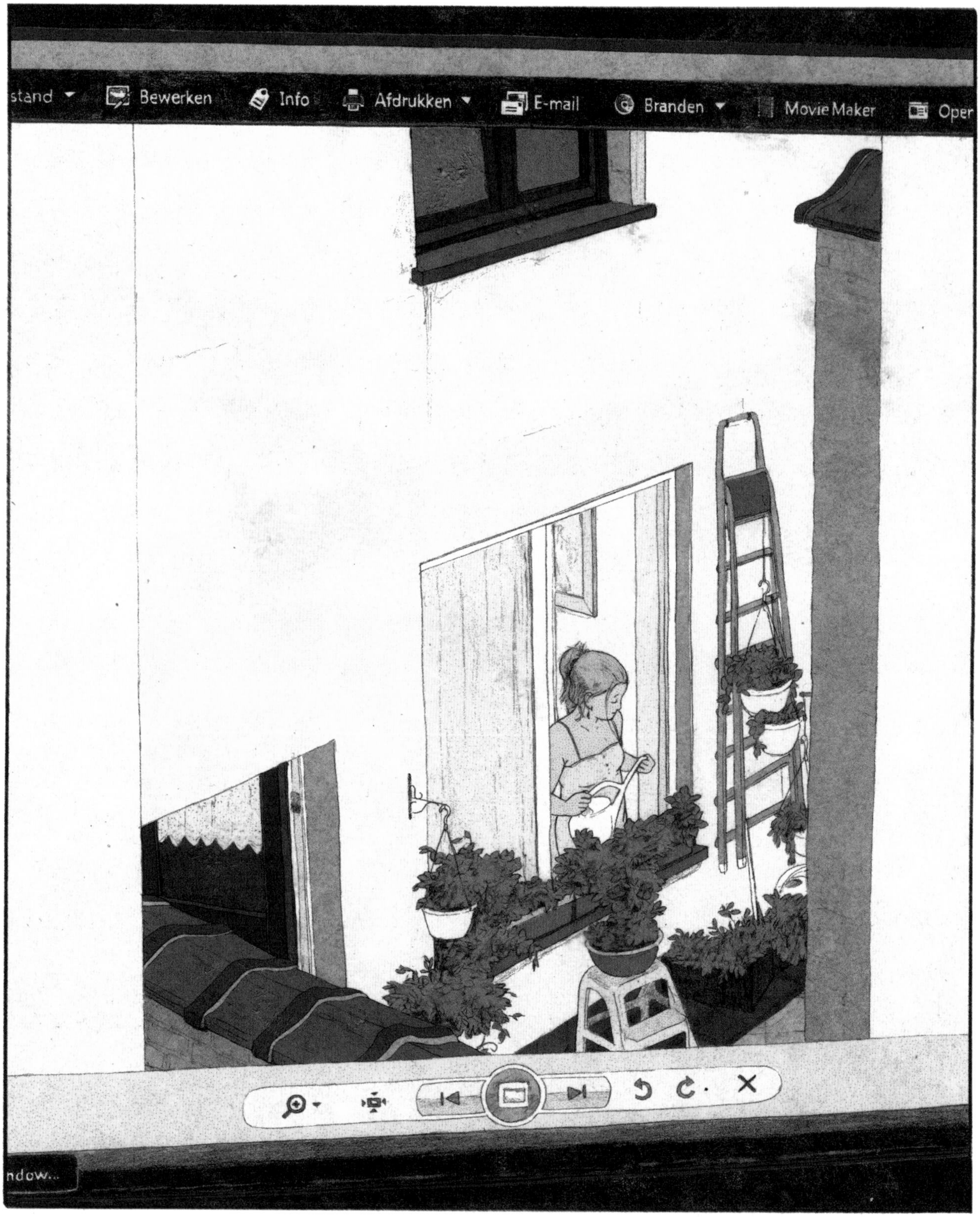
stand
Bewerken
Info
Afdrukken
E-mail
Branden
Movie Maker
Oper
ndow...

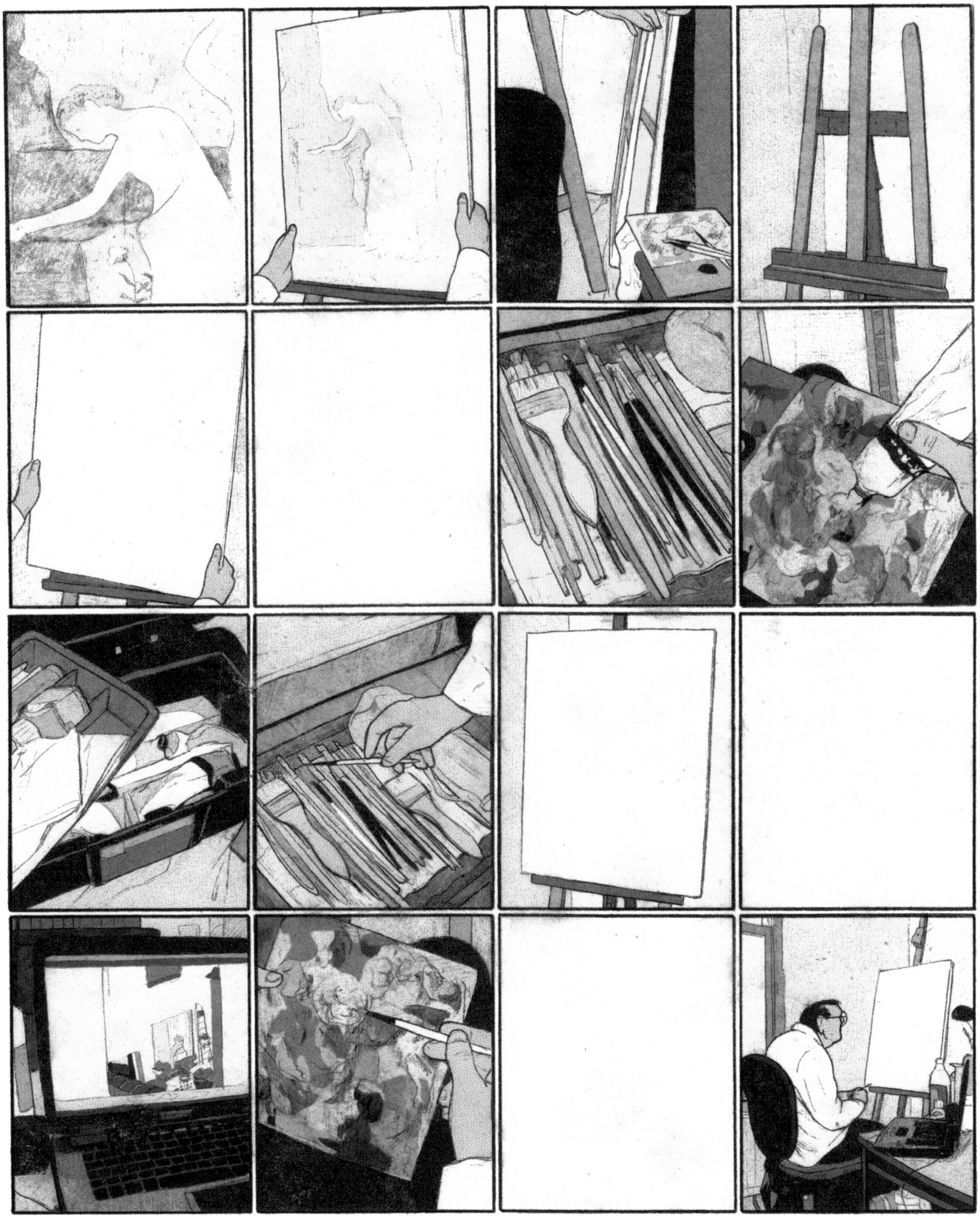

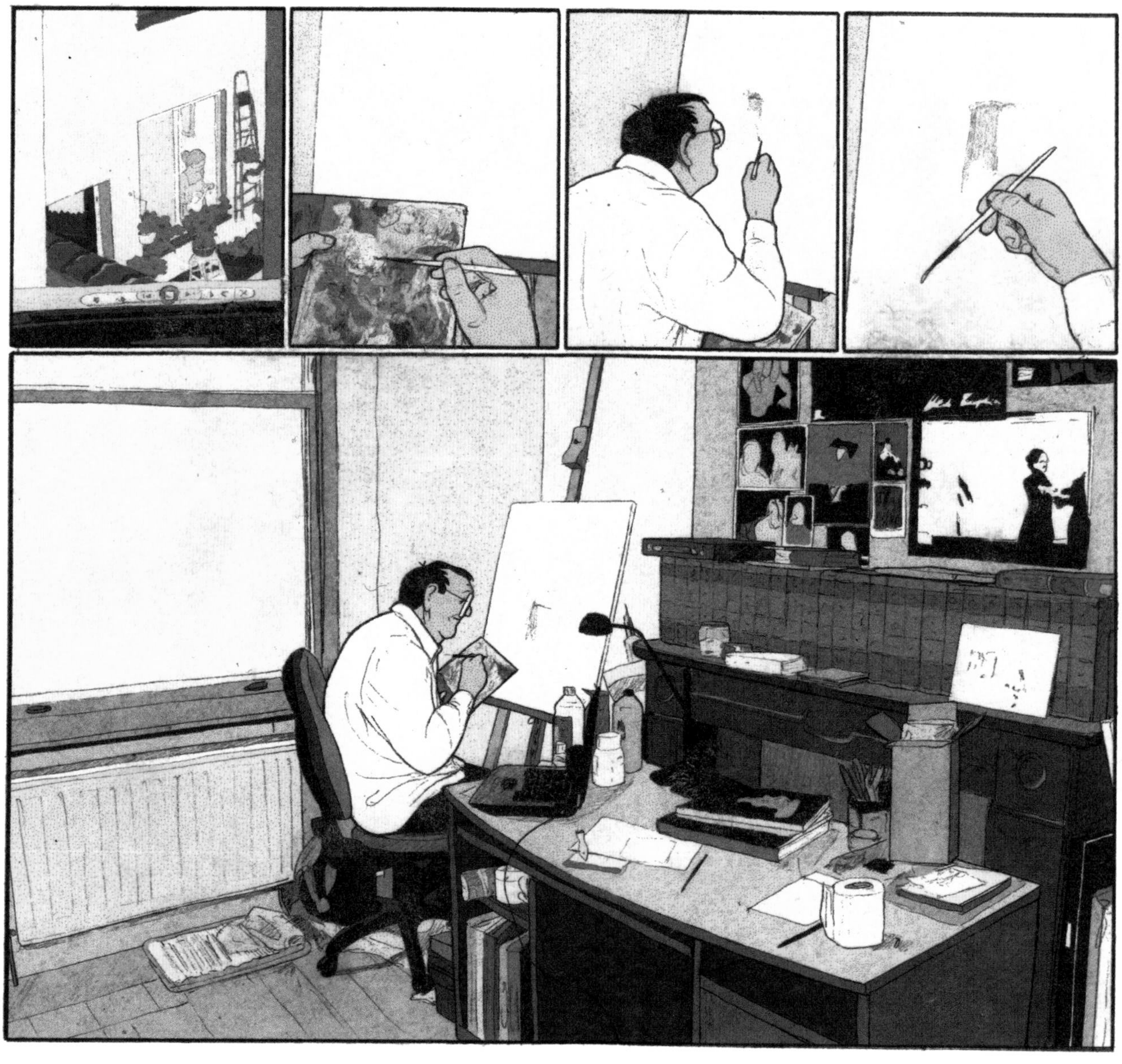

Ben Gijsemans (Lier, 1989) studied audiovisual arts at the School of Arts in Ghent (Gand) and then comics at the Hogeschool Sint Lukas in Brussels. He received an honorary prize for the first part of *Hubert* during his master's year.

I want to thank the wonderful people who were involved with the creation of this book: Fiona and Bram for posing whenever I asked them to, without making a fuss. Diede for his help with the dialogue, Johan and Nicolas for good advice along the way and the Flemish Literary Fund for giving me the financial help I needed in order to tell this story. Ben

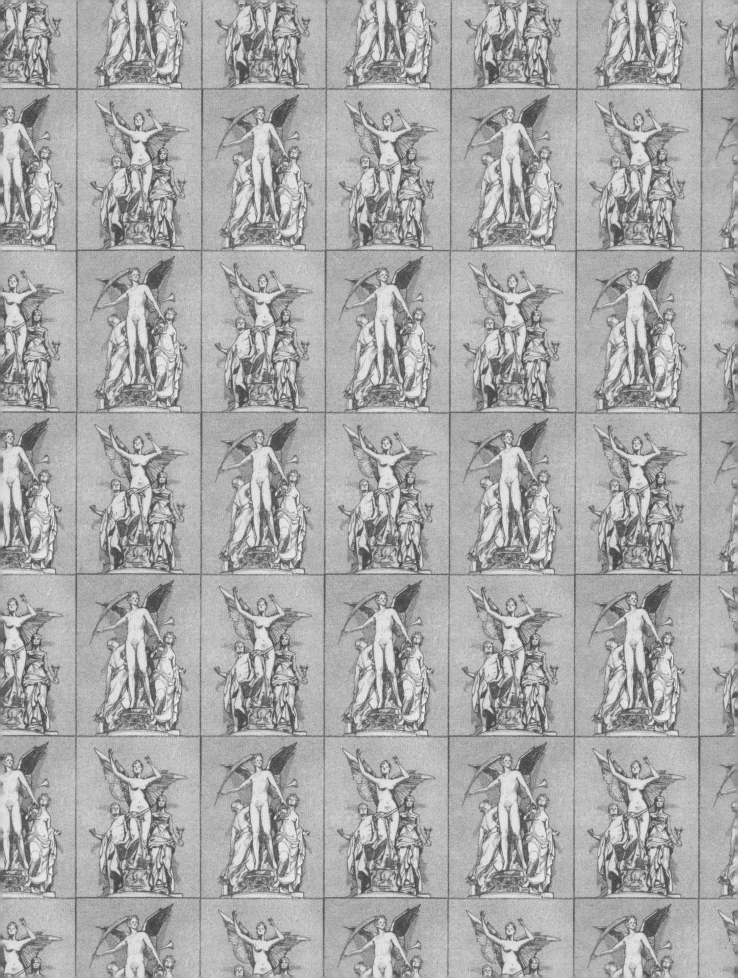